THE
Lost Treasure of
KING
JOHN
THIRD EDITION

WRITTEN BY
RICHARD WATERS

First Published in Great Britain in 2003
Text © RA Waters
All rights reserved
Second Edition Published in Great Britain in 2006 by TUCANN*books*
Third Edition published in Great Britain in 2014 by TUCANN*books*
Design © TUCANN*design&print*

ISBN Nº 978-1-907516-33-7

Published by: TUCANN*design&print*, Unit 9, Blackthorn Way, Five Mile Business
Park, Washingborough, Lincoln LN4 1BF
Tel & Fax: 01522 790009 • www.tucann.co.uk

CONTENTS

LIST OF ILLUSTRATIONS

———— • ————

ACKNOWLEDGEMENTS

———— • ————

Source material and other references are called up in italics, and listed in the bibliography.

I would like to thank the staff of the following organisations for their assistance in my research; The Library Services of Lincolnshire and Norfolk County Councils. The Sites and Monument Records/ Historic Environment Records of Cambridgeshire and Norfolk County Councils and especially Lincolnshire County Council. The Archives of Lincolnshire County Council, and the Collection (Lincoln's museum). The Royal Archives, and the Libraries and Archives at the Universities of Nottingham and Cambridge. History and Archaeology Faculty staff at the University of Nottingham. The Archivist at Worcester Cathedral and staff at Westminster Abbey.

Thanks to the staff at the Borough Council of King's Lynn and West Norfolk's Old Gaol House in King's Lynn, for kind permission to reproduce the photograph of the stunning King John Cup (Figure 18). Also to Rene Mouraille, the Newark and Sherwood District Council Ranger in charge of Newark Castle, for inviting me to visit and photograph the room in which it is believed King John died, (Figure 12).

The 3D visualisation of the Wellstream estuary (Figure 6) was kindly developed and supplied by Keith Turner at Working Pictures Ltd. Antiquus Reconstruction. The photograph of the Priestly Cross (Figure 17) was supplied by American correspondent Dean Smith. The photograph of the Templar tomblid (Figure 15) is borrowed from Tim Staniland's website www.thecyberfarm.com/templars. I am most grateful for consent to reproduce these images within my work.

A particular thank you to the owner of the property on which the effigy of Brother Simon presently resides (who wishes to remain anonymous), also to my former colleague Dave Cragg for his local knowledge, and to Prof. Malcolm Barber of the University of Reading for his interest.

Thanks to Tom Cann and his staff at Tucann, for all their work in formatting, printing and publishing this second edition, and particularly to Barrie Dunwell for the excellent cover designs on the past, and particularly the present, editions of the book.

Finally I would like to acknowledge the works and researches of earlier antiquarians, historians and authors who in their time have shared my interest in this subject, and to express my gratitude to all those people who, having read the first edition, took the time to contact me with further information and their own theories (in particular Margaret Bell for sharing her research into the de Gresley family), without all of whom this work could not have been as full.

R. A. Waters
2014

INTRODUCTION

—— • ——

O On the 12th of October 1216, King John of England reputedly lost his baggage train carrying supplies and great treasures whilst crossing the Wellstream between Norfolk and Lincolnshire.

Figure 1: King John

Following several years of casual research into this local historical curiosity, I read a brief account of the subject in a magazine article, which contained some major geographical inaccuracies[1]. This prompted me to finally sort out my various notes and to compile as full an account of the incident as I believed to be possible from the geographical and historical data available.

In the process of writing this account, I found myself also setting down various conspiracy theories, some of which had been in the back of my mind for some time, and some of which have evolved during the preparation of the account. I hope these are at least thought provoking to the reader, and whilst they may at times seem tenuous, should be considered within the context of the mediaeval period; an age when alliances between kings, nobles and agents of the pope could be forged or broken for personal gain, almost at whim.

Over the last eleven years, since the first edition, the book has sparked a pleasing amount of interest from a wide variety of people. In this third edition, as with the second, I have included some additional research and information, some of which has been inspired by those readers who have been kind enough to contact me with their own ideas, tales and information.

Interest has also come from local radio, Radio 4's 'Making History' programme, television documentary makers, and a couple of more unexpected directions too.

In 2005 I was asked by artist Adinda van't Klooster to contribute to the 'Sound Wall' project at Lincoln's new museum, The Collection. In 2009 I was asked by Canadian playwright Christopher Morley to proof read his new (and subsequently award winning) play 'The King's Disposition', which incorporated some ideas Chris had asked if he could borrow from my book. Both of these projects were enjoyable and very new experiences to me, and I am honoured to have been asked to make a small contribution towards them.

Sue Mortimer's book 'King John's Lost Treasure and the Templars' takes a thread from one of my theories and weaves a great fictional end into the historical fabric of the first part of her book.

It is now fast approaching 800 years since the events to be discussed in these pages, and it seems a fitting time to issue this third edition and perhaps awaken new interest in the subject of the lost treasure of King John.

– 1 –
THE WASH AND THE WELLSTREAM

———————— • ————————

Before looking at records of the event itself, it is worth considering the area in which it took place in order to set the scene.

The coastline of the Wash in Norman times was considerably different to that of today and can be approximately defined by the ancient sea defence known as "Roman Bank", much of which can be picked out on Ordnance Survey maps today and is shown on Figure 2.

Roman Bank has been said by many historians to be erroneously named. Instead of being Roman it is generally held to have been constructed around 1100AD[2]. The Domesday Book records the bank's existence in 1086[3].

However, finds of Roman coins and Romano-British pottery[4] in the parishes immediately behind the bank, tends to suggest that the name may in fact be correct. It is most likely that if the Romans settled the area, they would have undertaken some form of sea defence work, as can be witnessed by their extensive drainage works elsewhere in the county, such as the Carr Dike.

Roman Bank was constructed to protect a string of low lying settlements and grazing land around the Wash from inundation by the sea, and may well have been reinforced or heightened around 1100, which is at about the same time that a series of banks, known as dykes, were constructed inland to isolate good grazing land from the fens which were also prone to inundation when rivers inland were swollen by heavy rain.

The term dyke (or dike) is today often used to refer to the artificial watercourse (drain) created by excavating the earth used to build the bank, but it should properly be used to refer to the flood defence bank itself.

In plan, Roman Bank formed a funnel shape around the estuary of a tidal river called the Wellstream. On the west of the estuary lay Lincolnshire, and on the east, Norfolk, with Wisbech (Cambridgeshire) at the south entrance to the funnel.

The Wellstream no longer exists. Following various fenland drainage schemes, starting as early as 1478 with Bishop Morton's Leam, the River Nene was effectively re-cut from Peterborough to its outfall in the Wash, passing through Wisbech on the line of the Wellstream, and the whole surrounding drainage system established, which altered the previous natural system and environment beyond recognition.

The old River Nene had two outfalls; one into the River Wellstream at Outwell, to the south of Wisbech, and one into the estuary at Tydd Gote (from "Tide Gate"). The latter of these can be identified today with the course of Lady Nunn's Old Eau. It is likely that Nunn is derived from Nene. In Northamptonshire Nene is pronounced "Nenn" rather than "Neen".

At the time of King John, the estuary would have been silted up with outwash from the peatlands. The river outfall is likely to have consisted of several shallow channels seeking their way through the flats, as it could be crossed at low tide. This siltation can be deduced because it is known that in the latter part of the thirteenth century the Wellstream became silted up to such an extent that the river diverted itself at Outwell (just upstream of Wisbech) and merged with the Lynn outfall system[5]. In 1301 the diversion in turn silted up and the Wellstream again outfalled via Wisbech[5].

It is known that the estuary was passable even in mediaeval times, in relative safety, with the assistance of local guides, and was traversed between Sutton St. Mary (now Long Sutton) or perhaps, more precisely Sutton Crosses, south of Sutton St.Mary, in Lincolnshire, and Cross Keys (now Walpole Cross Keys) in Norfolk.

Sutton is thought to be a corruption of the Old English "Sudtun" or "Suptun", meaning South Town, and Crosses is thought to be from an Old Norse place name "Crossens", meaning headland with crosses[6]. Walpole is Old English meaning pool by the wall (sea bank)[6].

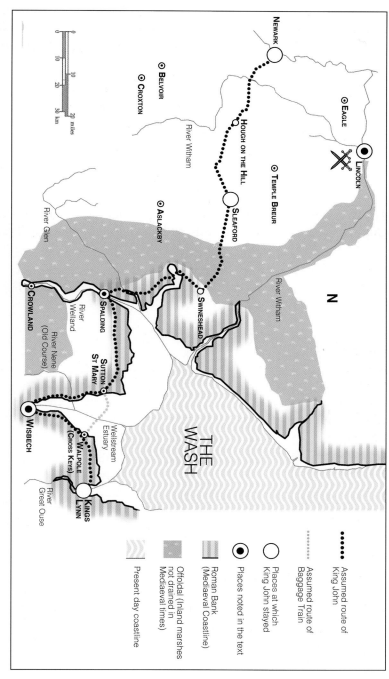

Figure 2: Plan of the Mediaeval Coastline of The Wash

It is likely that the Crosses were crossed keys (as with Walpole on the Norfolk side), meaning closed route, perhaps in reference to the symbol of St. Peter. Cross keys is a frequently used place name/public house name in the Fens, and its antiquity is testified by its use in later mediaeval times as a heraldic device in the Wisbech area.

In the time of Queen Elizabeth I, the route over across the *"Manor of Sutton marshes and sandes"* became recognised as part of the Queen's Highway. Passengers were escorted by guides and payment for this service was made to the *"Bailiffe of ye said manor"*[7].

The practice of crossing the tidal washes with the aid of local expert guides was maintained right up until the time of the final reclamation of the estuary in the 1820s (parts of the estuary having been reclaimed from the 1640s onwards). Figure 3 shows the gravestone in St. Mary's church, Long Sutton, of the last guide to the Wash crossing; Mr. Charles Wigglesworth.

As a result of the final reclamation of the estuary by the Duke of Bedford's land agent and land surveyor Tycho Wing in the 1820s, a large tract of agricultural land was created. Through this land, a straight outfall was cut for the tidal and navigable River Nene (already realigned upstream of Wisbech).

The land reclaimed by Tycho Wing was at one stage proposed to be a new county called Victoria. However, it became known as Wingland and following a lengthy meeting in October 1864, at the Globe Hotel in King's Lynn, the magistrates of Lincolnshire and Norfolk agreed to append Wingland, both east and west of the Nene, to the county of Lincolnshire[8].

In 1831, the first Cross Keys Bridge was completed, built in timber by the famous engineers John Rennie and Thomas Telford, over the River Nene, which with its approach causeways, directly links Long Sutton and Walpole. The bridge was replaced by a swing bridge in 1850, built by another famous engineer, Robert Stephenson.

The present hydraulic swing bridge was constructed in 1897 to allow for the passage of the new railway line over the Nene, and is still in good working order, although the former railway half of the bridge now carries

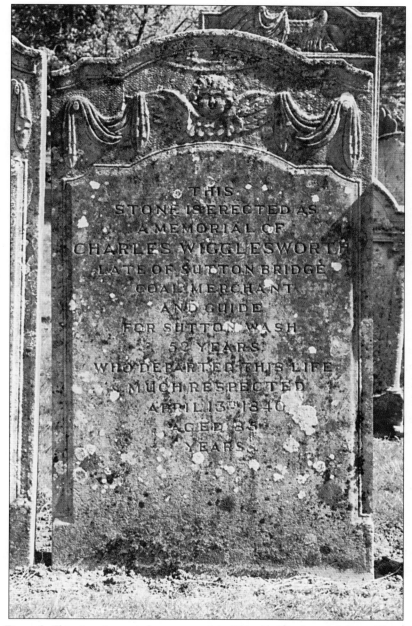

Figure 3: This stone is erected as a memorial of Charles Wigglesworth late of Sutton Bridge Coal Merchant and guide for Sutton Wash 52 years who departed this life much respected April 13th 1840 Aged 85 years

Figure 4: The Marshes at Gedney Drove End

the west bound carriageway of the A17.

From the above account of the changes that have occurred since the mediaeval period, it can be imagined that conditions in the estuary were very different to the agricultural environment of Wingland today. Figure 4, a photograph of the marshes of the Wash at nearby Gedney Drove End, illustrates the sort of treacherous landscape which would have existed before reclamation; a bleak marsh, criss-crossed with muddy, steep sided creeks.

It is very difficult once down on the marsh itself, to navigate, as there are no notable features apart from the sea banks themselves. One imagines that if viewed from half way across a six-mile expanse of similar terrain, even the banks would not be clearly visible. Firmish mud paths quickly become very slippery when wet, and it is easy to become stuck in the mud when trying to cross the creeks cut through the flats by the tides. These creeks, which wind their way through the landscape, rise quickly with the incoming tide and cut off large tracts of the marsh.

These conditions, especially if combined with rain or fog, make venturing on to the marshes of the Wash today, and certainly in mediaeval times (when there was the added obstacle of the Wellstream to cross), extremely hazardous.

– 2 –
PINPOINTING THE INCIDENT

—————— • ——————

When I first started collecting information about King John's treasure, my ambitious, and perhaps naïve, eventual goal was to identify a possible site at which the incident occurred, and at which there might be a chance of recovering something. I did not at that time realise how widely known the legend was in South Holland (the south eastern part of Lincolnshire), or indeed in north Norfolk and northeast Cambridgeshire, or how many people living in the area have opinions as to where the treasure may be.

My proposed method of identifying a potential site, was to attempt to find a possible route of an early causeway and a possible route of a main channel for the outfall of the Wellstream, the intersection of these being the point at which a change in the tides would have the most crippling effect on a column of packhorses crossing the estuary.

A preliminary study of 1:50,000 and 1:2,500 Ordnance Survey maps whilst compiling the map of the area shown in Figure 2, revealed some interesting place name clues, which I will discuss further later in this chapter, but gave me no help in my quest for early causeways or pre-drainage river alignments.

In the fens, the remnants of some earlier river courses can sometimes be detected and are known as riddons or roddons. Often these are clearly visible from the air as different coloured bands of soil, or as belts of more lush coloured crops, because the old depressions have gradually filled with finer quality topsoil.

Some former creeks and tributary systems are very clearly visible in the fields within parts of the Wingland using a well-known and freely available on-line mapping/aerial survey website. However, following many years of intensive agriculture (and dependent upon the season and weather conditions in which the aerial photography took place) they only present a very fragmented snapshot of the whole system of ancient watercourses. Tantalising evidence, but like a jigsaw with the majority of the pieces missing.

A more detailed desk study of various pre-1830 maps[9] and books on fenland drainage and folklore was largely unfruitful. A map in the Gough edition of Camden's Britannia (1789)[9(i)] shows a dotted line linking Sutton St Mary and Walpole Cross Keys. This line however was shown as straight, thus, whilst indicating that the estuary was traversed, I had to assume it was diagrammatic only. Guides would not have been necessary to negotiate a straight line, and it is unlikely that the nature of the estuary would have physically allowed the evolution or creation of, and maintenance of, a straight route.

The Badeslade (1723)[9(v)] and Cory (1793)[9(vii)] maps also indicate a track, slightly curved, across the estuary, which was by that time a narrower crossing than the mediaeval one, owing to successive reclamation schemes. Other maps including the very early Gough map (circa 1360)[9(ix)], indicate that a crossings existed by naming the minor settlements of Fosdyke and Walpole, but not the larger settlements such as Wisbech, thereby implying them to be of importance to travellers.

The maps referred to, show no consistency in the mapping of the Wellstream outfall, which implies either that the representations are again diagrammatic, as some clearly appear to be, or that the position of the main channel(s) shifted from time to time, which is very likely. In either case it was impossible to determine any specifics except that the northerly course of the old River Nene joined the estuary on the Lincolnshire side, as previously discussed in Chapter 1.

In conjunction with the desk study, I examined the area on site looking for any clues that may help my quest. The former estuary is now flat agricultural land with few distinctive features other than the present sea bank, Roman Bank, and the remnants of some banks which date from between the mediaeval period and the 1820s. There are numerous farms and small settlements but these are by definition relatively recent.

Roads and watercourses constructed within the former estuary are generally in straight lengths. There are some winding roads, which are generally slightly raised above the surrounding field levels. These winding roads often follow the routes of old sea banks constructed after Roman Bank and before the 1820s.

Two of these raised roads are of some interest as they cross each other at approximate right angles. The crossing of the two banks is most unusual as each successive generation of sea banks was constructed parallel to the previous one to reclaim a further strip of land. Furthermore, they are both lined with mature trees, which is quite distinctive in this environment and would indicate that both banks have existed for, I would estimate, around two hundred years.

The north-south running New Road clearly marks an old sea bank as it runs parallel to others, whilst the east-west running Avenue Farm Road is more curious. It may be constructed on an earlier causeway across the estuary. If this is the case, it is the only clearly evident example of such a route remaining today.

Driving along these roads I was fascinated to find that at their intersection was one of the place names of interest that I had noted during my desk study; King John's Farm. Figure 5 shows the position of King John's Farm and other sites relevant to the account.

Local folklore places the loss of the treasure at, or near, King John's Farm, built in 1878. Reputedly, the value of land in this vicinity has always been at a premium for this reason.

A further local tale is that King John's Farm is so named because the King stayed there overnight[10]. Although this is clearly impossible, as not only had the farm not been built, but the land on which it stands was still within the tidal estuary, it does serve to strengthen the association of the place with King John, and possibly stems from a corruption or misinterpretation of the treasure incident legend.

Another place name link, adjacent to the farm, can be found at King's Creek, which, unlike most of the local drainage system, follows an apparently natural meandering route giving it some antiquity. Perhaps this is the remains of one of the main outfalls of the Wellstream. Interestingly, the term "creek" is usually reserved for the watercourses meandering through the marshes beyond the sea bank, and I can think of no other

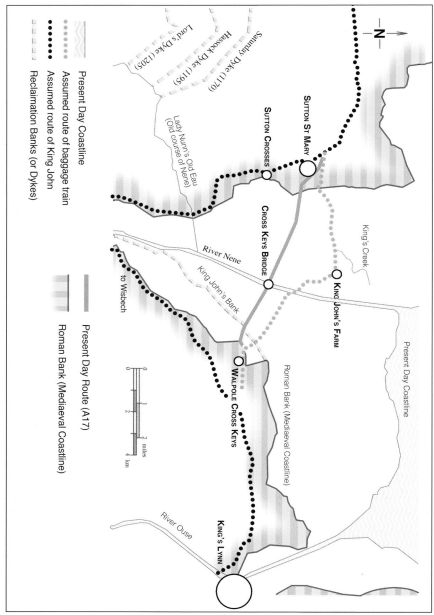

Figure 5:
Plan of
Wingland

example of an inland, non-tidal watercourse in Lincolnshire bearing the name creek, except for the nearby Westmere Creek, which further suggests its course predates reclamation.

W.Marrat states that the treasure was lost *"near a creek and a house occupied by Mr Mumby, called King's House in Sutton Marsh"*[7]. There is no King's House in the vicinity today, as far as I can determine. Perhaps this house was an earlier building on or near the site of King John's Farm.

G.Fowler[11] suggests that the farm is named after John of Gaunt who held land in the region. However, whilst this cannot be completely ruled out, it is unlikely, as this specific area had not been reclaimed during the lifetime of John of Gaunt (1340 to 1399), and given the extent of local folklore associated with King John and the close proximity of the creek, which Fowler does not explain convincingly, is most likely to be an attempt by Fowler to discredit the farm area in favour of his own preferred site for the loss of the treasure, near Wisbech.

Despite the origin and destination points of the guides, the routes implied on the early maps, the Elizabethan reference, the place names, the local folklore, and the fact that the Old Washway Road (a place name clue in itself) terminated at Sutton St. Mary, some earlier historians and scholars, particularly those of the mid nineteenth century[12], have proposed the crossing point to be much nearer to Wisbech.

However, if that were the case, the risks involved in the crossing would start to outweigh the benefit of the saving on distance. Consider that nearer to Wisbech, the Wellstream main channel(s) would be likely to be deeper and wider than those smaller channels threading their way through the silted delta beyond. Also, a supply column of the required magnitude, crossing at the narrow end of the estuary would probably stretch from bank to bank, making the total loss of the baggage train highly unlikely.

G. Fowler places the incident at the site of a ford between Walsoken and Wisbech, and states that there is no recorded evidence of a crossing over the estuary before 1700[11]. However, the suggestion of a crossing place offered by the Gough Map (1360), and the accounts of near contemporary chroniclers (discussed in detail in Chapter 4), together with the inscription on the gravestone of Charles Wigglesworth (Figure 3), stating him to have been the "*last guide*" between Sutton St. Mary and Walpole Cross Keys, indicates that their was a crossing before 1700.

The ford which existed between Walsoken and Wisbech was approximately 40 yards accross[11], which would make the total loss of the baggage train highly improbable. Fowler goes to some lengths to minimize the likely size and significance of the column, in order to justify his theory, and is backed up in this view by Professor James Holt.

Holt states that in 1212 the King's travelling court was typically supported by five packhorsemen and four carters[13]. This does not mean that the same was true in 1216, in a time of war, and certainly would not provide the logistical support necessary for the large retinue of mounted knights which the King had with him when he left Lynn (the supply column is discussed in greater detail in Chapter 4).

I suspect Holt may have favoured a crossing point north of Wisbech but south of the A17 in the Tydd Gote area; the reasons for my suspicions will be discussed in Chapter 10. This route would be something of a compromise between other routes, offering some saving on distance/time but at a position in the estuary where the far bank would have been visible (in good weather).

Author William Smethurst and marine scientist Jacqueline McGlade, have, more recently, postulated that the treasure was lost crossing the Welland estuary, not that of the Nene[14]. This idea has cropped up from time to time in the past, and appears in some cases to be based primarily on the similarity between the names of the River Welland and lost River Wellstream.

The attempts to substantiate the Welland theory are flawed by the failure of Smethurst to understand that the two rivers are different, and to appreciate practical details of the journeys undertaken by King John, and by his baggage train, which are explored in some detail in Chapter 4. This is strange, because Smethurst has clearly carried out a great deal of research into the area and into the subject matter, as witnessed in his fictional work which revolves around the treasure[15].

All things considered, in order to maximise the benefit of taking the risk of crossing the estuary, and taking into account the hints offered by the

Cross Keys and Washway Road place names and the early maps, it is my belief that guides escorted people across the marshes between Walpole Cross Keys and Sutton St. Mary (or Sutton Crosses).

If there is an actual site for the loss of the treasure, King John's Farm/ King's Creek, as well as being the obvious place name choice, is favourable in terms of the local geography. It is not far from the modern direct causeway (the A17) and the dotted line shown on the 1789 map[9(i)] associated with start and finish "cross keys" place names. It is easy to imagine a guide carefully picking his route across the marshes, having to follow any naturally higher banks of mud and avoid wetter areas, running sands and deeper creeks, and so having to deviate from taking a direct straight line route.

Of course, I am not the only one who has attempted to pinpoint the incident, there have been many before and will be many more. Some others have gone on to try and recover the treasure at their favoured locations, and some of those attempts are looked into in detail in Chapter 10.

Figure 6: Visualisation of the Mediaeval Wellstream Estuary. Reproduced by kind permission of Working Pictures / Antiquus Reconstruction

3
THE AMASSING OF KING JOHN'S TREASURE

———— • ————

Having looked in some detail at the historical geography of the area, the following chapters examine what the treasure may have consisted of, records of events leading up to the incident, and what is known of the movements of King John.

In spite of the success later attributed to the signing of the Magna Carta in 1215, in setting the law of the land, the barons of England were still in open revolt against the King and had invited Louis, Dauphin of France (later to become Louis VIII), to take the English throne.

Louis had already taken Normandy from John, which was one of the major concerns of the (Norman) barons of England. They effectively had to choose between their interests in England or their estates in Normandy, to side with the King of England or of France. To install Louis as the English King would allow them to retain their properties on both sides of the Channel[16].

Pope Innocent III, in 1212, had nominated Louis future King of England, having issued a declaration that King John was to be deposed. This followed a five year dispute between Pope and King over who had the right to appoint a new Archbishop of Canterbury, during which England had been placed under interdict and John excommunicated. The Archbishop elected by the Pope in 1207, Steven Langton (of the Lincolnshire village Langton-by-Wragby), only returned to England after John surrendered the crown of England to the papal legate, Pandulph, in May 1213 which resulted in the cancelling of the planned French invasion.

In May 1216, Louis landed in Kent and set about seizing England without papal consent, and was himself excommunicated, as were those who had invited him and paid homage to him at Dover; the rebel English barons and the Scots King Alexander II. The future of the English monarchy was very uncertain at this time and the King must have had to make some careful plans to face such a range of forces.

It is known that on 24th June 1215, within days of the signing of the Magna Carta, the King wrote to the Knights Hospitaller, the Knights Templar, and various religious houses, requesting the return of all royal possessions in their custodianship[18].

The Templars had already handed over the royal regalia and crown jewels of Lady Empress Matilda (King John's grandmother), on 28th May 1215[18]. It is known that as a result of the King's instruction, the Hospitallers released another set of royal regalia and crown jewels[18], possibly dating from King Alfred[19], on 26th March 1216, and that twelve religious houses also returned collections of items with which they had previously been entrusted[18].

It is known that the above collection was stored at King John's main repository at Corfe Castle[18] in Dorset, pictured in Figure 7. It is reasonable to deduce that they were removed by him during his stay there from 23rd June to 17th July 1216, or possibly on his visit there in 25th or 26th August 1216[20].

It has been suggested by some historians[21] that King John would not have carried his treasure around with him under any circumstances, and that it would all have been stored at Westminster. But as has already been noted, records exist of the distribution of treasures to various custodians throughout the kingdom for safekeeping, and as will be discussed later, what treasure was kept at Westminster Abbey was not lost.

A.V. Jenkinson's fascinating research work[18] on the inventory of known items within the collection is very specific and detailed. The following paragraphs are just a summary of the contents.

The Regalia of Lady Empress Matilda included a great crown, a purple tunic, a stone embroidered belt, shoes, gloves, a dark purple royal pallium (vestment) and dalmatic (robe), a gold broach, silk cloth, a sceptre and gold wand, the Sword of Tristram, another sword, a gold cup, and a gold cross. I have omitted the extensive descriptive work on jewellery, enamelling, and embroidery.

The second set of crown jewels included a sceptre, a gold wand, a red belt with precious stones, several other decorative belts, a jewelled collar, a

Figure 7: Corfe Castle, Dorset

red samite jewelled tunic, gloves, sandals, shoes, eleven pairs of basins, and various items of jewellery.

The treasures returned by the twelve religious houses included 143 cups, 14 goblets, 14 dishes, 8 flagons, 5 pairs of basins, 40 belts, 6 clasps, 16 staffs, 52 rings, 2 pendants, 4 shrines, 2 gold crosses, 3 gold combs, a gold vessel decorated with pearls (a gift from the pope), 2 candelabras, 2 thuribles (incense containers), 3 gold phylacteries (amulets or religious relics), and various other silver and jewelled items.

The King is also known to have had four rings presented to him by pope Innocent III in 1205, these being set with emerald, sapphire, garnet and topaz.

It is not known for certain why the King decided to gather these treasures together, or why he withdrew them from Corfe Castle. Perhaps he could no longer trust anyone else enough to have them out of sight; perhaps he was afraid of Corfe falling to the French or the barons in his absence, and opted to take his valuables with him.

It is quite possible that John needed the treasure to pay for the loyalty and service of his own fighting force, who were frequently paid in arrears at the end of a campaign, but could become disaffected if payment was held back for too long. Perhaps he intended to recruit foreign mercenary forces to reinforce him in his struggle to quell rebellion, and repel Louis. It was not uncommon for mediaeval kings to use their Regalia and treasures as collateral for loans to fund campaigns.

King John had resorted to using royal treasures to pay for his forces at least once already; in June 1216 he instructed Hubert de Burgh to use the royal plate housed in Dover Castle, to pay the King's troops besieged there[13].

It is also known that on the 18th October 1216, on his deathbed, the King sent a force of 300 Welsh troops to one of his commanders, Savaric de Mauleon, with a letter confirming they had been paid upto and including the 21st October[13].

If the above were true, the loss of the treasure in the Wash would provide a convenient excuse for its disappearance. This, I have called Conspiracy Theory No.1, as it turned out to be the first of several.

The main argument against this theory is that, as will be seen in the accounts of the chroniclers, far more than the treasure was lost. If the King had traded these treasures somewhere along his journey in October 1216, he would not also have lost all his other supplies, and the personnel, which accompanied them.

Whatever King John's reason for amassing the treasure and removing it from Corfe, what is apparent is that it does not appear as a complete collection in written history again.

Its disappearance would seem to be substantiated as the chronicler Matthew Paris notes[22], by the fact that John's son and successor, Henry III, was crowned at Gloucester on 28th October 1216, with a simple gold band and no noted royal regalia.

Matthew Paris does, however, also mention a later full dress ceremonial coronation for Henry III at Westminster, on Whitsunday 1220 where he notes that Empress Matilda's regalia were used[22]. The inventory for this regalia differs from that of the items handed to King John by the Templars some five years earlier. No mention is made of jewelled adornments and embroidery or of specific items, such as the Sword of Tristram.

It is documented that a crown and robes were taken from Corfe Castle to London, for the occasion[11]. This crown has been referred to as the "*German Crown*"[23], which could have been an alternative name for Empress Matilda's crown, denoting her Germanic origins.

The implication could be that either the regalia used in 1220 were hastily assembled replacements for the documented set, or, that Empress Matilda's regalia were not part of the treasure lost in the Wash at all.

A logical explanation for the use of the simple circlet crown at the original coronation of Henry III, in 1216 is that, at the age of nine years old, the young king was simply too small to wear a full crown. This does not explain the discrepancies between the original regalia of Empress Matilda and that used in 1220, or why there are no subsequent inventories of crown jewels which make mention of Empress Matilda's Regalia, the Crown of Empress Matilda, or the German Crown, including an inventory of 1250 during Henry III's reign.

It is recorded that for the coronation of Henry III's son, King Edward I, in 1272, and in all subsequent mediaeval coronations, the regalia used was that of Edward the Confessor, last used at his own coronation in 1042 and subsequently bequeathed to the nation for the use of future monarchs[23].

This regalia had been stored as a complete collection at Westminster Abbey and its inventory differs extensively from the sets discussed above, except that the crown in the Regalia of Edward was reputed to be that of Alfred the Great. The crown survived until the Commonwealth inventory of the disposal of the Crown Property of Charles I in 1649, and is recorded several times up until that event as "*the Crown of Edward*" or "*the Crown of Alfred*"[23]. It is interesting to note that the second set of regalia listed by Jenkinson[18], and possibly attributed to King Alfred does not include a crown.

The Tower of London holds no records of items lost by King John in the crossing of the Wash, but has a traditional understanding that three quarters of his treasure did not return[24]. This is very vague and is perhaps based on the knowledge that the regalia of Alfred the Great and Empress Matilda were lost, whilst the regalia of Edward the Confessor was not.

To summarise this fairly complicated situation regarding different coronation sets, it would appear likely that King John withdrew from Corfe Castle, in addition to the collections of treasures reclaimed from the religious houses and various personal collections and miscellaneous treasures, the full Regalia of Empress Matilda, and also the Regalia of Alfred the Great (excluding his crown which had previously been incorporated into the Regalia of Edward the Confessor, and was thus housed separately).

Whilst the Regalia of Empress Matilda was, according to Paris, used for the second coronation ceremony of Henry III, it does not appear to match the earlier inventory. The Regalia of Empress Matilda, the Crown of Empress Matilda and the Regalia of King Alfred disappear from record between 1216 and 1250. As King John was transporting them around the countryside in 1216, the assumption of Jenkinson[18] that they constituted part of the treasure reputedly lost in the Wash, does not seem unreasonable.

In the events immediately preceding the loss of the treasure, King John had, on 3rd Sept 1216, issued a proclamation from Oxford to rally his supporters. He re-took Cambridge from the rebel barons a fortnight later and then made his way north into Lincolnshire[25].

The King and his army fought in the defence of Lincoln Castle, which was held by his cousin Nicola de la Haye, between 28th September and 2nd October 1216, against the rebel army.

Nicola, whom King John made High Sheriff of the County of Lincoln during the last five months of his reign, outlived two husbands, the second of which was Gerard de Camville, Lord of Sutton Holland Manor, who had commanded King Richard's fleet of ships on crusade, and to whom King John had given a charter to hold a market at Sutton St Mary in 1202. Following the death of her husband in 1214, Nicola spent a lot of time at Sutton St Mary[7].

When the King arrived in Lincoln on 28th September, Nicola, owing to her age, offered the King the keys to Lincoln Castle, but he begged her to carry on holding the fort for him, and she continued to do so.

The King then toured Lincolnshire, looting and destroying the estates of his disloyal barons, staying at Grimsby (3rd October), Louth (4th October), and Spalding (7th and 8th October), before proceeding to Lynn in Norfolk, where he arrived for the night of 9th October[20]. His arrival in Lynn was welcomed by the people and he was reputedly showered with gifts. Lynn later became known as Bishop's Lynn and then King's Lynn (after King John).

At Lynn, the King was to reunite with a further company of troops, which he had earlier dispatched to wreak havoc on the estates of rebel barons in Cambridgeshire and Norfolk. The successful result of this tactic was to panic those barons, who were engaged in the siege of Windsor Castle, drawing them away and thus lifting the siege[16]. Undoubtedly a side benefit was the seizure of further treasure as a result of the looting, to add to John's hoard.

As an aside, King John's 1216 battle at Lincoln Castle was not the end of the story for Nicola de la Haye. After John's death she continued to defend the castle against a seven month siege by the forces of English barons Robert Fitzwalter and the Earl of Lancaster, who were later heavily reinforced by the French army under the command of the Comte de Perche and the Marshal of France.

On the 20th May 1217, the army of the young King Henry III, led by his regent William the Marshall, 1st Earl of Pembroke and still regarded as the greatest knight in England, arrived at the North gate of the city, that approach being chosen so that the army did not have to battle up hill to reach the castle. The English leaders of the Anglo-French siege force wanted to come out and meet the English army in open battle, but the French Marshal insisted on them remaining within the shelter of the city walls.

The Bishop of Winchester, Peter de Roches (one of the executors of King John's will) knew that the west gate to the city had been blocked up in the past, but that it could be breached, and so the relief force stormed in from the north and the west. The Anglo-French force was forced into bloody hand to hand combat in front of the castle and cathedral and was also under crossbow fire from Nicola de la Haye's castle defenders, as illustrated in figure 8.

During the battle, the Comte de Perche was fatally speared through his visor but managed to strike three severe blows to the helmet of William Marshal before falling from his horse. William survived. As the battle progressed, the Anglo-French troops were driven down Steep Hill into the lower town and routed[26].

After the battle William Marshall's forces went on to loot and sack the city of Lincoln, the citizens having supported the barons and the French over the preceding two years. This event has become known as Lincoln Fair.

The battle was the decisive victory in the war against Louis, and marked the end of the French campaign in England. It is said that many fleeing French soldiers were killed by peasant folk between Lincoln and London as they tried to make their way south in an attempt to leave the country.

After the battle Nicola was relieved of the office of Sheriff and also of her hereditary post of Castellan of Lincoln Castle, however after travelling to court to personally appeal against this, the castle was returned to her custodianship. She continued to serve as Castellan until her death in 1230[27].

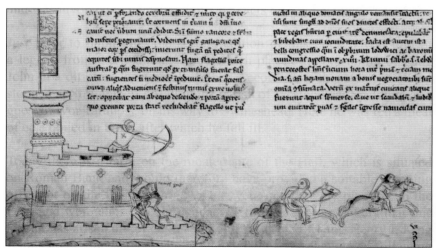

Figure 8: The battle for Lincoln Castle (from Matthew Paris's Chronica Majora; circa 1259)

4
THE LOSS OF THE TREASURE

────────── • ──────────

On Wednesday 12th October 1216, King John and his army left Lynn for St. Mary's Abbey at Swineshead in Lincolnshire (Figure 2). He is known to have visited Wisbech on the same day[20].

The King may have taken the road from Lynn to Walpole Cross-Keys (which runs north of and parallel to the present A17) via Clenchwarton and Terrington St. Clement, riding on ahead of his baggage train. At Walpole Cross Keys he is likely to have turned south and followed Roman Bank to Walsoken, where the Wellstream could be crossed, to Wisbech. He cannot have travelled along the erroneously named King John's Bank, as it is thought not to have been constructed until the 1640s.

Alternatively he may have diverged from the route of his baggage train earlier in his journey, at West Lynn, and taken the road southwest to Walsoken via Terrington St. John and Walpole Highway (which runs roughly along the route of the present A47 as far as Walton Highway).

At Wisbech, the King is recorded as having engaged the services of eight shipmen to carry *"goods and merchandise"* to Grimsby[28]. It is likely that this was to reinforce, or provide supplies to, his troops at Grimsby, but the thought that this cargo may have been the treasure supposedly lost the very same day in the Wash has crossed my mind, and certainly didn't escape the attention of some of the earlier investigators into the incident, including Gordon Fowler, who thus arrived at a similar theory to my Conspiracy Theory No.1 (that the treasure was disposed of by King John possibly as payment for troops).

Fowler[11] includes an interesting translation of the King's letters drafted at Wisbech, demanding safe passage for the boatmen; *"The King to all etc. Be it known to you that the goods and merchandise which are in the ship which Ralph Fitzwalter brings to ours; we have ordered them to be brought to Grymesby. And therefore we command you neither to do nor to allow to be done any harm or hindrance to the said Ralph or to the goods or merchandise on board his ship. These letters are to be valid from Friday next (14th October) after the feast of St. Denis in the 18th year of our reign and for eight days after. Witness myself at Wysebeche, 12th October in the 18th year of his reign."* A matching letter was issued for the other seven boatmen; Godfrey le Pohier, Osbert Fitzwalter, Benidict de Beaupre, Thomas de Beautre, William the German, Reginald But and John Fitzalan.

James Wright puts forward a suggestion that the boats may have been commissioned to transport the treasure to Wellow Abbey near Grimsby, where, he states, the King had a good relationship with the abbot[29]. There is no further justification for this idea.

W.H. Warren dismisses the suggestion that the boats carried away the treasure from Wisbech, because not only do the letters make no mention of where the ships were lying, but they are also post-dated by two days. This implies the boats were lying elsewhere and not expected to depart for two days. It is possible that the purpose of the diversion to Wisbech was specifically to catch up with these carriers or contacts of theirs, to complete the transactions started with them at Lynn, possibly to arrange transport of the winter supplies John had acquired for his northeastern strongholds[28].

Professor Holt[13] notes that the fact that the boatman's letters were prepared at all, and the fact that the patent rolls form the period leading up to and following the incident have survived intact, shows that the King's scribes and whatever their means of transporting their records was, did not perish in the Wash, but travelled with the king.

Whether the King would have travelled via Wisbech, had it not been for his business with the boatmen, is open to conjecture, but Wisbech would have provided suitable accommodation for refreshment and perhaps a change of horses on his journey. The King was certainly familiar with the locality and had traversed or circumnavigated the Wellstream estuary a few days earlier, on the 8th October, on his way to Lynn, and also on at least one previous occasion, on 8th October 1205.

On reaching the Lincolnshire side of the estuary, the King is again likely to have followed Roman Bank north to Sutton St. Mary, fording the old River Nene's northern outfall on route.

Roman Bank, a remaining part of which is pictured in Figure 9, is likely to have been used as a causeway in preference to routes across the marshes inland. It was dry, safe, solid, and virtually straight, whereas the tracks inland were little more than cattle droves for access to pastureland, many of which were (and some still are) dead ends.

Figure 9: Roman Bank, Looking North to Sutton Crosses

On reaching Sutton St Mary, the King would have taken the Old Washway Road west to Holbech and then to Spalding, where the tidal River Welland could be forded. He would then have travelled north to Swineshead, skirting round Bicker Haven (another now reclaimed tidal estuary).

He is known to have lodged at Swineshead Abbey on the nights of the 12th, 13th, and possibly the 14th of October 1216[20].

The distance from Lynn to Swineshead on the route proposed above is about 40 miles, which whilst a considerable journey for a single day, was not out of the ordinary for King John and his court, as can be found by studying the King's Itinerary[20].

According to the chronicler Roger of Wendover[30], the King had with him a force of *"two to three thousand mounted knights"*. Such an army would require a considerable retinue of squires, servants, footsoldiers, archers, armourers, smiths, and cooks, together with supplies of food, weaponry, drink, and personnel such as courtiers, advisers, holy men and the King's own bodyguard. All of this would be necessary, with or without a collection of treasure, and the predominant means of freight transport was still the packhorse.

It has been calculated that such a supply train would be in excess of two miles long, moving at an average speed of two and a half miles an hour[31]. It would thus take 16 hours to complete the journey from Lynn to Swineshead without rest or disruption.

Clearly it was not a practical proposition for the baggage train to keep up with the King, and it is very likely that their journey was intended to take two days, the 12th and 13th of October, with a possible rest day on the 14th. The available daylight hours in October would make an eight hour travelling day plus time to set up and break camp, more practical than a 16 hour day. This would explain why the King stayed at Swineshead for two or three nights, at a time when he was under pressure to keep moving. This is a pattern repeated often in the King's Itinerary[20].

For the lumbering supply train, a saving of up to nine miles (three and a half hours journey time) could be made by opting to cross the Wellstream estuary, between Cross Keys and Sutton St. Mary, a distance of five miles as the crow flies, as opposed to 14 miles travelling along Roman Bank via Wisbech.

Ralph of Coggeshall[32] wrote; *"Moreover, the greatest distress troubled him, because on that journey (from Lynn) he had lost his chapel with his relics and some of his packhorses with divers household effects in the Wellestream, and many members of his household were submerged in the waters of the sea, and sucked into the quicksand there, because they had set out incautiously and hastily before the tide had receded."*

Calculations have been carried out[33] to show that low tide on 12th October 1216, would have been around 12.00 noon, which would have been a little after the arrival of the baggage train, tending to support Ralph of

Coggeshall's record. Undoubtedly soft silty mud and running sands, which could be misinterpreted by some as quicksand, were present in the estuary, as in the Wash marshes today.

Fowler[11] refutes the presence of actual quicksand, based upon a technical description of "*wet quicksand*"; and whilst he is strictly speaking, quite correct, such scientific or prescriptive definitions would not have been in existence in mediaeval times.

Interestingly, calculations have also been carried out, which have shown that low tides between the 12th and 14th of October were also the lowest tides of the year and therefore the optimum time for making such a crossing. This suggests the King and his advisors had given some detailed advanced planning to the campaign.

A second chronicler, Roger of Wendover's account[30] of the incident is as follows; "*Then heading for the north, he lost by an unexpected accident all the wagons, carts, and packhorses, with the treasures, precious vessels, and all the other things which he cherished with special care; for the ground was opened up in the midst of the waves and bottomless whirlpools engulfed everything, together with men and horses, so that not a single footsoldier got away to bear tidings of the disaster to the King. The King however, barely escaping with his army, spent the following night at an Abbey called Swineshead.*"

With regard to reliability of these chroniclers, it is clear from comparing the accounts that either Ralph or Roger, or both, were not eyewitnesses. Their descriptions of the losses suffered and the actual nature of the cataclysm, differ greatly. Ralph's description is the least fanciful and mentions quicksand and timing of tides, which as shown, were real problems, as opposed to the bottomless whirlpools of Roger's account.

Roger's account also seems to be confused as whether the King himself, was present during the incident. To have "*barely escaped*" implies that he was present, but the lack of survivors able to bring him news, implies that he was elsewhere. This tends to support the evidence that he travelled via Wisbech with his knights and at least some of retinue (those clerks who prepared the letters for the boatmen).

Both accounts were laid down in the early 1220s and are therefore not strictly contemporary with the event.

The only other known chronicler who is roughly contemporary to mention the event is Matthew Paris[22], however his record was laid down as late as the 1250s, a generation later, and is basically an embellishment of Roger of Wendover's account, with the significant additions that the crossing was attempted without a guide, and specifically mentioning the King's diversion via Wisbech.

These later facts are either from a different source or are interpretations of Matthew's own device, based on later knowledge. It would certainly have been foolhardy to have attempted the crossing without a guide, and the diversion to Wisbech is cross-referenced by the King's Itinerary[20].

With or without a guide, if the vanguard strayed off the safe path, or an incident occurred which crippled a wheeled vehicle, a single file column would be paralysed, and if it had travelled a sufficient distance from the Norfolk bank, would not only be unable to continue, but would also have insufficient time to return to Walpole Cross Keys before the tide came in.

S.A. English gives an excellent and detailed account of the logistics of crossing the marshes, with regard to the timing of the arrival of the column at Walpole Cross Keys and the timing of the tides and means of crossing, which point to the possibility that if the baggage train arrived at the crossing say two hours later than planned, or got lost in crossing due to the lack of a guide thus delaying the completion of the crossing by two hours, all would indeed have been lost, and it would be likely that all personnel would have perished[16].

E.W. and B.A. Robinson[7], and more recently Sue Mortimer[34] have also written good imaginative accounts of how the disaster might have occurred whilst crossing the marshes with their treacherous hidden creeks, which give due consideration of the type of transport, local geography, and tides, present at the time.

G. Fowler makes an interesting study of stolen tides[11], which are accompanied by an eagre (tidal bore) and bring a high tide two hours early at certain times of the year. This would provide a devastating natural explanation for the incident, as the creeks would have been filled up almost instantly on the passage of the tidal bore, cutting off anything that had not been physically washed away by the eagre itself. Local fishermen and the guides are likely to have been aware of these natural phenomena, and of their timing, which is generally associated with exceptionally high tides. As previously noted, calculations suggest exceptionally low tides on the date of the incident, and low tide around midday, therefore this explanation must be considered to be unlikely.

As previously noted, the Welland has been confused with the Wellstream by some researchers. W. Smethurst has resorted to redating the King's departure from Lynn and visit to Wisbech to the 11th of October, so that the timing of the crossing of the Welland could be achieved around noon on the 12th, in order to justify his theory[14].

Local historian Nigel Panting suggests that the King had an overnight stay at Wisbech on the 12th October, to similarly justify the timing of a crossing of the Welland, but on the following day[35]. E.W. and B.A. Robinson think that the King may have overnighted at Sutton St Mary on the 12th October[7]. None of these redating theories are supported by the Itinerary of the King[20] or any other corroboratory evidence.

At this stage in my investigation, thoughts of deliberate sabotage, either as a military stratagem by the barons, or as a get rich quick ploy by the local guides, started to form in my mind. It would most certainly have been possible for a guide to deliberately mislead the column if he wanted to, later spreading the rumour that the baggage train had set off without a guide, or at the wrong time of day to cross before the tide came in again. This early suspicion of foul play forms my Conspiracy Theory No. 2.

If the incident had been deliberately staged by guides, the motive would be more likely to be strategic and at the instigation of others, rather than for personal greed. Retrieval of any goods would have had to wait until the next daylight low tide and would have been somewhat risky, if there had been anything left to retrieve. It is also most unlikely that peasant folk would dare attempt something of this nature, even if the King was hated by much of the populace of the country, without the protection of someone of influence.

Robert de Gresley (or Grelley) was the fifth Baron of Manchester, and also Lord of Swineshead. His ties with Swineshead and in particular the abbey, are discussed in Chapter 5. He was one of the six northern barons who instigated the baron's revolt against King John[36]. He would have had a detailed knowledge of the estuary and its crossings, as he regularly traversed between his estates in Swineshead and Sixhills in Lincolnshire, and Tunstead in Suffolk.

De Gresley had sworn loyalty to King Richard I, and in 1199 to King John. He had supplied armed knights for the service of both Kings for royal campaigns in Britain and France, but in 1213, he and five other barons, refused to support John's planned campaign to Poitou, as they felt their resources would be better employed defending their English territories against the Scots, Welsh and Irish[17]. Also, they would be aware of the Pope's plans to replace King John with the Dauphin of France, and would not want to support John in a campaign against the French.

De Gresley is included in Matthew Paris' list of *"presumptuous and fiery"* leaders who took up arms against the King at Stamford. He was present at the signing of the Magna Carta, and the day after, was entertained by King John at Windsor Castle where he was gifted with the King's deer to stock his own estates, and with land at Bilsthorpe in Nottighamshire[17].

Magna Carta did not resolve the unease between the barons and the King, and by December 1215, Robert de Gresley had his lands confiscated. On two occasions in 1216 he was, along with the other rebel leaders, given the chance of safe passage to negotiate with the King, but refused to attend. He was amongst those who paid homage to Louis of France when he laid siege to Dover Castle, along with King Alexander II of Scotland.

Certainly Robert de Gresley had the motives, means, local knowledge and contacts to orchestrate the deliberate severance of the King's supply column from his army. This would have been a deft military manoeuvre and would have had a devastating effect on the King and his forces, who were already under pressure on so many fronts.

— 5 —
KING JOHN'S STAY AT SWINESHEAD ABBEY

———•———

According to Roger of Wendover[30], King John did not receive news of the incident in the Wellstream estuary until he had reached St. Mary's Abbey at Swineshead on the evening of 12th October.

The shock discovery of the loss of support for his knights, the possible loss of infantry, archers, other personnel, and all supplies including his personal wealth, must have been devastating to the King in his struggle to quell civil war, particularly as according to Ralph of Coggeshall, messengers also brought news to Swinehead that his garrison at Dover was on the verge of surrender to the French forces[13]. During his stay at Swineshead however, the King suffered an even greater set back.

It is a well known Lincolnshire legend that one of the monks at the Cistercian Abbey of Swineshead, a Brother Simon, poisoned King John with new wine or cider spiked with toxin obtained from pricking a toad.

There are two equally recounted versions of the monk's motive for poisoning the King. The first being that the King had, whilst dining, asked how much a loaf of bread was worth in those parts, to which Brother Simon replied a ha'penny. King John's response, at first in jest, was to threaten to increase the price forty fold within a year, as a means of increasing his tax revenue. Having deliberated on the idea for a while, the King then put this forward as a serious proposition. Brother Simon was guilt ridden at the thought that his disclosure could result in the imposition of an unbearable tax on the people, and knew they would not be able to afford such an increase.

The second version of the legend has King John summoning the sister of the Abbot of Swineshead, a reputedly beautiful and chaste nun, called Judith, to the Abbey, and more specifically to his chamber. Knowing of the King's reputation and likely intentions, Brother Simon decided that something had to be done, if Judith's honour was to be saved.

In both stories, the monk sought, and was granted absolution, from William the Abbot, before carrying out his public spirited deed. The poison was served to King John in a drink, but Brother Simon was challenged to drink it himself before the King would accept it, as was the practice if a taster was not available (it is assumed that the King's taster had been lost in the crossing of the Wash). The monk took a draught then left the King to drink his fill, retiring to his cell where he died shortly afterwards. The King in turn, fell ill, but the monk's death was kept secret, so that his illness could not be associated with poisoning. King John died a few days later at Newark.

This legend is so widely known, and accepted as folk history, to many in south Lincolnshire, that it can not be dismissed out of hand, even though Roger of Wendover[30] attributes the King's death to *"gorging on peaches and new cider"*. Ralph of Coggeshall[32], again taking a more logical view of events, explains the King's illness as *"fired by gluttony at Lynn"*.

As cider enters both the Swineshead legends and Roger's account, it may be worth mentioning that October is the correct time of year for cider making, and that as with most alcoholic drinks at that time, it was frequently made by monks and drunk, largely for sanitary reasons, in preference to water. East Anglian counties including Norfolk have a tradition of cider making which may have extended north into Lincolnshire in the middle Ages when the drinking of cider was far more wide spread in England. It is said that a local variety of apple known as the Kirton Pippin, produced good quality cider[37]. Cider apples are still commercially grown in the area, particularly to the north of Wisbech.

It is also worth noting that the monks of Swineshead had a vested interest in the price of bread, as a large part of their livelihood was derived from the income of Manchester's mill. This was granted to them by Robert de Gresley, first Baron of Manchester and Lord of Swineshead, who was also the founder of Swineshead Abbey in 1134[38]. This Robert de Gresley was the ancestor of Robert de Gresley, fifth Baron of Manchester, who continued to grant the income of the mill of Manchester to the monks of Swineshead. If bread were priced out of the reach of the people, not only would the people suffer, but the income of the Abbey also.

At this stage in the investigation, the intriguing coincidence of the King's death being within seven days of the loss of the treasure becomes even more suspicious, because potentially, the King was actually poisoned on the night of the 12th October, the same day as the incident in the Wellstream, or at least before leaving the Abbey on the morning of the 14th or 15th. This inevitably, leads to the casting of some suspicion on the Abbey.

Could it really be possible that the monks of Swineshead could have poisoned the King of England, making up the very feasible story that he was ill with dysentery on his arrival? If so, would they have had the means to intercept the baggage train, before its arrival at Swineshead, or to manipulate the incident in the Wash, keeping the treasure for themselves? If the monks colluded with their dispossessed benefactor, Robert De Gresley, he could have resolved the logistical problems of waylaying the baggage train for them, as suggested in Conspiracy Theory No.2. This idea forms my Conspiracy Theory No.3.

This theory has some fundamental problems. The main ones being that the King did not die immediately after the poisoning, and would surely have suspected some foul play. Also, the Cistercian brethren were sworn to a simple life of poverty and would, at least on the face of things, have no need of a vast material wealth (this of course would not apply to Robert de Gresley, if he were involved in the conspiracy). The possibility of a holy man committing murder, let alone of an Abbot giving approval for the act, would seem to be unlikely in the extreme.

That King John would be suspicious of poisoning is not necessarily the case, remember that he witnessed Brother Simon taste the drink and retire from his presence in apparently good health.

The abbey is shown on the Badeslade map (1723)[9(v)] as *"the Abby where King Iohn sickned"*. The word poisoned is not used but the implication is that the onset of illness did not take place before arrival at Swineshead.

King John was grossly unpopular with the Cistercians owing to his taxation policies. He was the first English monarch to tax religious houses, and it is known that the nearby Abbeys of Crowland and Peterborough had been *"sorely molested"* by his taxation.

It is recorded by the chronicler of Crowland Abbey[39] that the establishment was actually looted by King John's army, being *"miserably destroyed and even the sacred vessels carried off"*, probably in retribution for its support of local rebel barons.

Some Cistercian houses had been forced to close, the monks being reduced to begging in order to survive, making John even less popular both in the eyes of the people, and of the wealthy, who's donations of land and monies helped to establish and maintain religious establishments.

A monk at the Cistercian Abbey of Revesby, some 13 miles from Swineshead, is recorded as having been arrested for *"his part in the wars against King John"*, but was released because his offence had been committed after he had become a monk[24]. I am unsure as to why his status of monk absolved him of whatever he is supposed to have done wrong. The offence is not disclosed and cannot therefore be directly linked to events at Swineshead, but perhaps this was a man who new something of the events surrounding the death of the King.

It is interesting that Shakespeare, writing around 1596, was aware of the poisoning legend, as he has King John poisoned by a monk at Swineshead Abbey, and adds that the monk, *"a resolved villain"*, tasted the drink first and subsequently his *"bowels suddenly burst out"*[40]. The discussion in the script implies that the monk's death was public knowledge, as he died in the abbey farmyard, and that the King was aware that an assassination attempt had taken place. However, Shakespeare places the King's death at Swineshead, which shows that he was using some poetic licence in his writing (as may be expected of a playwright in order to economise on scene changes). That fact that he was aware of the legend at all in the late sixteenth century is, I feel, of significance in itself.

Raphael Holinshed's *"Chronicle of England"*, compiled in 1587, is widely accepted to have provided the background information for Shakespeare's historically based works, but the source for the play *"King John"* is believed to have been an anonymous chronicle/historical drama called *"The Troublesome Raigne of Iohn King of England"*, first published in

1592[41]. This drama in turn appears to have drawn on fifteenth century accounts.

William Caxton's chronicle[42], printed in 1480, is the earliest account I have identified which contains reference to poisoning at Swineshead as the cause of the King's death. This is clearly the source material for a series of other chronicles, such as the St Albans "*Brut*" from 1483. John Foxe's "*Book of Martyrs*" (1583 edition) collates some of these accounts and includes a woodcut in story board format entitled "*The Description of the poysoning of King Iohn, by a Monke of Swinestead Abbeye in Lincolneshire*"[43], this can be seen in Figure 10.

Caxton's chronicle contains detailed similarities to both the local legend and Shakespeare's play. As in legend; the monk is named Brother Simon, asks for consent form his abbot, who "*much commended hys fervent zeale*", and it is stated that three monks sang mass for his soul everyday after his martyrdom. Similar to Shakespeare; the monk had a "*wicked heart*" ("*resolved villain*"), and died with "*his guts rushing out of his belly*" ("*bowels suddenly burst out*").

Brother Simon's motive in Caxton differs from legend, as the monk is said to have taken offence at the way the King spoke of Louis, the Dauphin of France[42].

None of these later chronicles are in any way contemporary with the events in question, in contrast with Roger of Wendover and Ralph of Coggeshall. This implies that either the local poisoning legends had become widely accepted by 1480, and subsequent chroniclers felt bound to record them despite the two earlier ecclesiastical chronicles to the contrary, or that the poisoning story was known by clerics to be the historical truth, but had not been recorded as such before (at least in any known earlier chronicles), perhaps for political reasons.

Whilst the thought of the monks of Swineshead Abbey poisoning the King seems a little fanciful, these were violent times and assassination in some form or other is not at all beyond the realms of possibility. In addition to religious houses, the King was unpopular with many others, especially the feudal landowners of England, due to his constant tax raising efforts, including shield tax to fund defensive and offensive wars on various

The Defcription of the poyfo
of Swineftead Abbey

Figure 10: The Poysoning of King Iohn (From John Foxe's Book of Martyrs; 1583)

ning of King Iohn, by a Monke
e in Lincolneshire.   Place this in page. 2 5 6.

fronts, and his demands for soldiers to mount these campaigns. He was also unpopular with the Irish, the Welsh, and the Scots, all of whom he had tried to subjugate with varying degrees of success. His relationships with the main powers in Europe, the French crown, and the Pope were unstable.

In King John's defence, it should be noted that owing to his lack of popularity amongst the landed and the religious (the only literate classes); history has undoubtedly painted a very biased picture of him.

On receiving the throne, John also took on a massive debt from his brother Richard's crusading exploits. Ironically, King Richard I is painted as an English hero, when in fact he spent less than nine months of his reign in England. John on the other hand, interspersed with periods of absence defending his interests in France, particularly his hereditary seat in Anjou, and short campaigns in Ireland, toured England relentlessly, ensuring the crown court at which he presided, provided a uniform system of justice throughout the land. The briefest study of the King's Itinerary[20] shows that King John did not take his responsibilities to the country lightly; instead, he travelled the nation almost constantly.

Having spoken in John's defence, he was undoubtedly a cruel and calculating monarch. He is said to have personally murdered his nephew Arthur of Brittany in order to secure his right to the throne of England, and was involved in many cold blooded acts during his reign.

Just prior to publishing the second edition of this book, I was told of a legend from the Spalding[44] area which places the poisoning of King John in a different location altogether. According to this story, the King stopped at St. Lambert's Hall in the parish of Weston near Spalding, as a guest of Ivor Taillbois, on his way to Swineshead. Here he was fed a meal of eels boiled in broth after which he fell ill.

Today there is a farm on the moated site of the Hall, which is situated on Roman Bank and would therefore have provided a suitable stopping off point on the King's journey. Eels were undoubtedly plentiful in the Fens and were considered a delicacy. However it seems likely that this legend has arisen out of confusion with the death of King Henry I, King John's great grandfather, who is widely believed to have died following consumption of a *"surfeit of lampreys"* in 1135 (lampreys being a parasitic fish similar in appearance to eels).

My belief that this tale is a corruption of the Henry I story is supported up by the fact that Ivo de Tailbois (or Taillebois), Baron of Kendal, having come to England with William the Conqueror in 1066, married a noblewoman of Spalding and then founded a Benedictine priory near Spalding in 1085 (having harassed the monks of the pre-Norman Spalding Priory of St. Mary's to such an extent that it ceased to exist)[45]. His descendant in King John's reign was Ranulph Tailboys[46]. Therefore Ivo would certainly have served Henry I but was not a contemporary of King John.

– 6 –
THE LAST DAYS
OF KING JOHN

———— • ————

On either the 14th or 15th of October, King John left Swineshead. The Itinerary of the King[20] does not record where the King spent the night of the 14th; it could either have been his last night at Swineshead or spent on route to Lafford (Sleaford) Castle, where he is known to have stopped on the night of the 15th.

When he left Swineshead, he was in such a poor state of health that he had to be carried on a litter. Whilst staying at Sleaford the King was reputed to have made a slight recovery following blooding (the mediaeval cure-all practice of leeching), however he was on the road again the following day as the Itinerary[20] shows that he spent the nights of 16th, 17th, and 18th of October at Newark Castle, pictured in Figure 11, and thus his condition deteriorated once again.

Both Sleaford and Newark Castles belonged to the Bishop of Lincoln, Hugh of Wells. Hugh was present at the signing of Magna Carta. Henry I granted their construction circa 1135, by the then Bishop of Lincoln, Alexander de Blois (also colourfully known as Alexander the Magnificent).

Although the King is supposed to have reached Newark on the 16th October, local tradition says that he spent a night at Hough-on-the-Hill[47] shortly before his death. I would suggest that this was the night of the 16th, either at the castle or the small Augustinian priory which existed there, and that he then preceded to Newark on the 17th.

Wendy McConnell[24] cites a Robert de Brunne, as recording a traditional belief that the King's death took place at Hough, but this is not supported by the chronicler's detailed accounts of events at Newark Castle.

Hough is nine miles from Newark and almost exactly the same distance from Sleaford, thus forming an ideal half way stop over for the ailing King on his litter, which must have been slow and uncomfortable.

Figure 11: Newark Castle

It could be said that the very fact that no wheeled vehicle was available to carry the King of England goes some way to showing that his supply column had indeed been lost.

Wendy McConnell[24] suggests that the King may have died several days before reaching Newark, possibly at Swineshead, and quotes the phrase "*bowels burst forth*" as a possible description of bowel relaxation after death or a literal explosion following a build up of gases due to several days of decomposition. However, the phrase quoted, if taken from Shakespeare's "*bowels suddenly burst out*" is written specifically in respect of the death of Brother Simon, not the King. McConnell does not speculate as to why the corpse would be taken all the way from Swineshead to Newark without first being treated, but the theory is highly unlikely owing to the accounts of leeching and slight recovery at Sleaford, and detailed accounts of events such as the making of a will at Newark.

At Newark Castle, the King dictated a will naming his executors; these included Gualo (Papal Legate), Peter de Roches (Bishop of Winchester), William the Marshall (First Earl of Pembroke), Ranulph of Chester, Savaric de Mauleon and Falkes de Breaute (two mercenary captains who had been loyal to the King). The executors were instructed to "*make satisfaction to God and the Holy Church for the wrongs I have done them*", to send aid to the Holy Lands, and to offer alms to the poor and to religious houses[25]. A wish list guaranteed to smooth his passage to

Figure 12: Newark Castle Gatehouse

heaven. William the Marshall was also nominated to act as regent for the King's eldest son Henry, whom he declared heir to the throne.

As mentioned in Chapter 3, it is also recorded that on the 18th he dispatched a contingent of Welsh troops to de Mauleon, with a letter stating that they had been paid.

49

On the night of 18th October 1216, Adam the Premonstratensian Abbot of Croxton, administered the Eucharist and performed the last rites for King John. In the early hours of the 19th October, King John died of food poisoning, or of dysentery, at Newark Castle.

It is thought that the King died in a room directly above the main gate, pictured in Figure 12, as this was the only room in the castle known to have had a fireplace and chimney at that time[48]. The exterior masonry of the gatehouse visible today is Tudor, but this masks earlier Norman masonry, the remains of which are still visible between the Tudor window openings from the inside of the room. It is believed that the gatehouse and keep were combined at Newark at the time of King John[48].

It has been said that the body was examined by a surgeon, and no traces of poison found[38], but I doubt that the symptoms of the two potential causes of death would have been distinguishable in mediaeval times.

The surgeon was Adam of Croxton who was said to have been a skilled physician. Adam removed the King's heart, ring finger, and intestines[48]. It was common practice for different parts of deceased monarchs to be buried and venerated at different locations, and these organs were taken by Adam to Croxton Abbey, in Leicestershire, where the ring finger and heart were buried beneath the high alter, and the intestines buried beneath a pagan burial mound in the Abbey grounds[48].

The removal of internal organs, particularly evisceration, had the very practical purpose of reducing the effects of putrification of the corpse, which in King John's case had to be transported all the way to Worcester for burial.

When Adam attended to the corpse, he reputedly had to cover it with his own gown, as the body had already been looted of everything except the undergarments.

As an interesting aside, it is claimed that earlier that same year, King John had visited Adam and had blackmailed him out of 400 marks, following an affair between the Abbot and a noblewoman of Croxton Kerrial[48]. If the blackmail story is true, perhaps Adam may not have exercised all his skills as a physician when he had earlier visited the King on his deathbed.

Figure 13: King John's Tomb in Worcester Cathedral

The story of Adam of Croxton's gown is borne out to some degree, by the exhumation of the king's body at Worcester Cathedral in 1797, when the skull was found to be covered with a monk's cowl. Figure 13 shows King John's tomb in Worcester Cathedral, which carries a marble effigy that originally formed the coffin lid.

An account by V. Green of the removal of the corpse in 1797 notes that the body was clothed *"similar to that in which his figure is represented on the tomb, excepting the gloves on the hands and crown on the head, which on the skull was found to be the celebrated monk's cowl"*[49]. The whole body was wrapped in a crimson robe which may possibly have been added when the tomb was disturbed during earlier alterations in 1529, when it is suspected that disturbance and exposure to light and air may have caused disintegration of some of the finer original garments[50].

Green[49] notes the presence of maggot remains within the mediaeval clothing, which were not specifically mentioned as being evident on the robe and the cowl. This has been interpreted by Wendy McConnell[24] as suggesting the cowl was added in 1529 with the robe. That there were no maggots mentioned on the robe or cowl specifically, does not mean that there were not any present. The robe would have trapped the insects within it, hence they were prevalent on the lower garments.

What is interesting about Green's account is that the corpse was buried with fine garments, including a sword and scabbard, but with no crown. A poem by J. Bale[51], written after the opening of the tomb in 1529, states that the corpse did have a crown, along with a rod and sceptre, which suggests that some regalia may not have been lost in the Wash, but it is difficult draw any conclusions when the two accounts differ on the issue of the presence of a crown. It is evident and understandable that Bishop Silvester of Worcester, William the Marshall and other assembled nobles ensured the King's body was interred with some dignified clothing, even if his own garments had been stolen at Newark.

The monk's cowl has given rise to the Worcester legend that the King had asked to buried disguised as a monk, so that he could trick his way into heaven, having been excommunicated by pope Innocent III in 1209, and also no doubt as a result of the poor reputation attributed to him since his death. This legend is more likely to be an explanation for the cowled corpse, rather than the true reason for it, as King John was reconciled with the Pope in 1213, and his excommunication revoked.

Following the death of the King on the 19th October, chroniclers record that *"wayfarers on the roads around Newark reported men and laden packhorses leaving the city"*. This, together with the near naked corpse, and the already recounted story of the coronation of Henry III, with a simple gold circlet, implies that anything which the King had left after the incident in the Wash was stolen by his courtiers and servants. The King's own bodyguard can have had little loyalty for their monarch, to allow, or even participate in, robbing his corpse of clothing.

The whereabouts of the *"two or three thousand mounted knights"* (less the three hundred Welsh troops previously accounted for) at this time is not mentioned, they may have already deserted the King, or they may be the men reported by the wayfarers, demobilising and returning to their homelands. It is possible that they, or some of them, formed the cargo of the Lynn boatmen, and that they parted from the King at Wisbech.

Could it be possible that the King's own courtiers, servants, or knights, were really responsible for the disappearance of the treasure, later telling the tale of the failed crossing of the Wash to backdate its disappearance, as a means of protecting their innocence? It is most likely that they were owed payment for their work during the ongoing civil campaign. This is my Conspiracy Theory No.4.

The major problem with this theory is that a conspiracy of this magnitude would surely involve too many self-motivated individuals, to have remained secret. From a practical point of view, as already noted, the King didn't have access to wheeled transport between Swineshead and Newark, which tends to suggest that the baggage train, and therefore presumably the treasure, was lost prior to leaving Swineshead.

It is evident that most of the King's personnel deserted him around the time of his death. It is likely that these people were the travellers noted by the wayfarers, some of whom may have participated in the theft of the King's remaining valuables and clothing. After all, the King was so unpopular that it may have been dangerous for his courtiers to have continued to show loyalty in public after his death, choosing instead to put some distance between themselves and the dead King.

One of the executors of King John's will, William the Marshall, without doubt the most trusted noble at the King's court and entrusted with the safekeeping of his son and heir, had been designated Custodian of the Royal Treasury by King Richard I on his deathbed in 1199[52]. William would have had a detailed knowledge of the treasure and the contacts necessary for its safekeeping or even disposal.

William's involvement in a conspiracy to appropriate the royal treasury has to be viewed as unlikely, as he was a loyal servant to Henry II, Richard I, John and Henry III (for whom he defeated the French at Lincoln as discussed in Chapter 3), until his death in 1219 at the age of 72. However, it remains an outside possibility and re-enters the story in the following chapter.

−7−
BROTHER SIMON

---•---

So far I have endeavoured to recount and correlate all the geographical and historical information available to me, surrounding the loss of the treasure, and the coincident death of King John. In the process of doing this, I have arrived at several possible alternative explanations for these events, but have never been quite satisfied with my theories.

Of course it could be the case, that King John lost his treasure in the Wellstream estuary and died of dysentery very shortly afterwards. However, I continued to view this series of events with some suspicion, and during my investigation into the legend of Brother Simon a surprise discovery triggered a further theory. This has evolved, during my writing, into my fifth and final explanation for the disappearance of the treasure; Conspiracy Theory No.5.

I had read that there was in Swineshead, a single piece of masonry, identifiable as originating from the Abbey[53]. Doubtless, much of the ordinary masonry had been looted for use as local building stone after the dissolution of the monasteries by Henry VIII, but this specific piece was of particular interest, as it was said to carry a carving of Brother Simon.

Thinking that this image would make an interesting photograph to accompany my text, I decided to find out if it still existed. Certainly it existed in 1791, as an account exists of a farmer having shot at its nose for pistol practice[54], and presumably, it still existed when written of in 1926[53].

I tracked the carving down, and it turned out to be a tomb effigy with the lower part of its legs missing, upended and built into the wall of a later structure. However, I was surprised to find that instead of being depicted as a monk, Brother Simon is clearly depicted as a knight, as can be seen in Figure 14.

Knowing that Swineshead was a Cistercian house, and that the Cistercian monks and the Knights Templar were in some way linked, I wandered if Brother Simon could have been a Templar knight.

I am informed that scholars from Cambridge have visited and studied the effigy, and have identified the general armour depicted as typical of a crusader knight, and the chain mail type as being specifically early thirteenth century[55], and therefore, exactly contemporary with the events in question. Unfortunately the Dept. of Manuscripts and University Archives at Cambridge University Library were unable to provide, or unwilling to look for, any background papers to this earlier research.

The flat shape of the head depicted, is a result of a hidden scull cap worn beneath the chain mail coif, and this is indicative of early thirteenth century armour. The narrow sword belt corresponds to this dating, as belts tended to increase from approximately 25mm to 75mm wide as the 1200s progressed[56]. The simple cushion further supports the early thirteenth century dating of the effigy. Double and pleated cushions being characteristic of later thirteenth and early fourteenth century effigies[56].

Figure 14: The Effigy of Brother Simon

The wavy lines used to depict the chain mail rings however, are more typical of later thirteenth century Lincolnshire and Yorkshire effigies[56], and Prof. Malcolm Barber of the University of Reading, a leading scholar of the Knights Templar, is of the opinion that the overall style of the effigy is no earlier than the late thirteenth century[57]. Pevsner's Lincolnshire also describes the effigy as late thirteenth century[58].

It was not uncommon for effigies to be added to notable tombs at later dates, or for recarving to have taken place from time to time and so dating remains open to interpretation.

An anonymous stone slab covered the majority of known early Templar graves, generally bearing a carved image of a Templar cross and/or a sword, such as the tomblid from the South Witham preceptory pictured in Figure 15 (this had been used as a footbridge over a ditch until its recent discovery). However, as the Order became wealthier, some notable Templar knights were honoured with full effigies as can be seen in the London Temple. One such effigy in the London temple is that of William the Marshall, First Earl of Pembroke and Custodian of the Royal Treasury, who was admitted into the order shortly before his death.

Figure 15: Templar Tomblid

It can be seen from the remaining upper parts of the Swineshead effigy's legs, that they would have been crossed, right over left. It is a matter of conjecture as to the exact meaning of the cross-legged representation of a knight.

In the eighteenth century, this was believed to specifically denote a Knight Templar, and this interpretation is still held as being correct by some[59]. The motif was later taken by others to denote any crusader knight who had seen active service, the cross legs being analogous with the cross.

It is possible that the crossing of the legs was nothing more than a trend amongst the sculptors, which became popular from around 1230[56]. Similar trends being to depict the hand drawing or holding the sword, from around 1275, and to depict the hands in prayer and legs straight, from around 1300[56].

Perhaps it is a coincidence that the lower part of the slab depicting the crossed legs is missing, or perhaps the slab was deliberately broken below waist level when it was saved from the abbey after the dissolution (when the rest of the fabric was being robbed for building stone), thus preserving the secret of Brother Simon's identity. It is difficult to imagine accidentally breaking such a large slab of masonry.

Templars were forbidden to shave their facial hair and kept their hair cut short. It is impossible to determine the hair length of the knight depicted in the effigy, owing to his chain mail coif, which also covers the majority of the beard area. There does not appear to be any facial hair but the face has been too badly damaged to say that the image definitely does not have a beard (the eyes and mouth have been crudely recut, presumably following the defacement in 1791). In any event, if he were masquerading as a Cistercian monk, he would have had to have had his hair and beard cut to suit.

Of course it is possible that the effigy represents some other contemporary local knight or noble who was buried in the abbey, such as the benefactor Robert de Gresley who died in 1230. The deaths of Robert de Gresley's father Albert, and son Thomas, do not fit in with the dating of the effigy. Albert and Robert de Gresley and others of their line are believed to have been buried under the parish church of St Mary the Virgin, of which they were also benefactors, and which dates back to at least 1201[38].

It has been suggested[24] that the image might represent Simon de Montfort, who was a later benefactor of the Abbey. However, de Montfort died at the Battle of Evesham in 1265; he was dismembered and denied a Christian burial by Henry III's son Edward. He has no tomb and hence there is no effigy of him.

The fact that the effigy was the only identifiable piece of masonry preserved from the Abbey suggests it was held in some esteem by the local people, who have continued to uphold the tradition that the image represents the martyr, Brother Simon, who poisoned King John.

The Templar Rule was established by Bernard of Clairvaux, head of the Cistercian order, and based upon the rule of that brotherhood[60]. Major J.W. Collinson gives a good concise summary of the Templar Rule, for further reading on the subject[61]. One of the abbots of Swineshead, Crilbert of Holland, was a friend and disciple of Bernard of Clairvaux[38].

There were some fundamental differences between the two orders, perhaps the greatest of which was that the Templars had papal consent to take lives in the interests of the church. For a Templar to kill an enemy of Christendom whilst on crusade, not only was he not committing a sin, but also could use such an act to atone for previous sins, including murder, which he might have committed before joining the brotherhood. *"Taking the cross"* (going on a crusade) could in itself revoke excommunication.

I think this alone is sufficient difference to establish that the Cistercian monks and the Knights Templar were not part of the same brotherhood, but they did develop in tandem, and had links sufficient enough for some historians to refer to the Templars as the military wing of the Cistercians. The two orders even followed the same rules in the running of their farm estates. Both orders began life as austere, chaste, anti-materialistic disciplines, and both accrued property and wealth as they evolved, which some historians have viewed as having corrupted their principles.

The financial status of the two orders at the time is of some interest. As previously noted, the Cistercians were suffering unprecedented taxation at the hands of King John, some houses being forced to close. Meanwhile the Templars' wealth continued to increase. The Templars' escalation of wealth internationally was such that the major monarchs of Western Europe were envious of, and perhaps intimidated by them[62].

The fact that the loyalty of the Knights Templar lay with the Pope, rather than the monarch of the country in which they resided, together with their wealth, lead to a degree of distrust in the them from the Kings of Europe. However, their skills as negotiators, bankers and military advisors gave them a valued civil servant type role within royal courts. They acted as international bankers to monarchs seeking monies for ventures in the Holy Lands, and as secure holding houses for the personal wealth of individuals, including monarchs, who were outside the brotherhood.

Much of the Templars' wealth came from the lands of knights who joined them, being obliged to renounce material goods and personal wealth. The Templars were also gifted by nobility, who sought to ensure their passage to heaven. Indeed William the Marshall is said to have died penniless. His admission to the order shortly before his death would explain this, and presumably the wealth he brought with him to the order explains his personal effigy and burial within the London Temple.

The motive for William's entry into the order just before his death, and following a lifetime of loyal service to the English monarchy, has puzzled me. Of course it could be the final act of a pious man, leaving his wealth to an order dedicated to recovering the Holy Lands for Christendom, but effectively it implies a switch of allegiance from monarchy to papacy. In light of William's position as Custodian of the Royal Treasury, and in respect of my Conspiracy Theory No.4, it would be interesting to know what wealth passed into the hands of the Templars at his induction into the order.

Having witnessed the merciless taxation of their Cistercian brethren, and fearing sequestration of their own wealth, or perhaps acting in the interests of the French crown and/or the Pope, it is surely within the realms of possibility that the Templars sent Brother Simon to Swineshead Abbey to assassinate the King. Brother Simon selflessly giving his own life for the greater good, and being buried at Swineshead with military honour, as implied by his depiction in the effigy. It is said that masses were offered to him for many years after the event[53], which would tend to support the local insistence that the effigy is definitely that of Brother Simon.

This theory would explain the folk tale of Brother Simon seeking absolution from Abbot William for his intended crime, which could be granted to a Templar but would be unthinkable for a Cistercian monk.

In addition to the motive of removing the threat to the existence of the Cistercian (and other) orders, the Templars would have had sole access to the royal treasury previously held by the twelve religious houses and their rival order, the Knights Hospitaller, as well as themselves.

The local tales surrounding these events, such as the proposed taxation of bread and intended molestation of the Abbot's sister, could have evolved in folk tradition as publicly acceptable explanations of the actions of the supposed Cistercian monk, rumours of which may have leaked into the public domain at a later date, to become accepted by chroniclers in the fifteenth century, as discussed in Chapter 5.

The story of the loss of the treasure in the Wash, may also have been invented to explain away its disappearance somewhere between Lynn and Sleaford, with such a dramatic and totally conclusive event that no-one would be able to question it.

If this theory seems a little tenuous, it is worth considering that the chronicler, which I have already identified as being closer to the apparent events by virtue of his accounts, Ralph of Coggeshall, was a Cistercian monk. He was the Abbot of Coggeshall from 1207 to 1218. Coggeshall Abbey has been described as the *"sister abbey"* to Swineshead, although I am unsure of the reasoning which might substantiate this connection.

Roger of Wendover, on the other hand, was a Benedictine Prior at Belvoir, in Leicestershire. As a point of interest, the rule of the Knights Hospitaller was based upon the Benedictine order in the same way that the Knights Templar were founded on the traditions of the Cistercian order. It is also a point of some interest that Belvoir is only a couple of miles from the Premonstratensian Abbey at Croxton, from which came Adam, the Abbot who attended King John's deathbed (refer to Figure 2).

It is likely that Roger's account was based upon information received via Adam. Certainly it is a logical explanation for the differences between the accounts of Ralph and Roger. You will recall that Ralph's account identifies the commencement of the King's illness at Lynn, thus placing Swineshead Abbey beyond suspicion. His account of the loss of the treasure in the Wash, although completely unverifiable by witnesses due to its totality, described the event in terms of realistic natural conditions within the tidal estuary.

Roger's account places the commencement of the King's illness at Swineshead; following the taking of rough alcoholic drink (poisoning is not mentioned). This may have been the apparently real course of events as recounted to Adam by those courtiers, ignorant of any conspiracy, who were still with the King at Newark. His account of the loss of the treasure is somewhat fantastical, and is certainly not based on first hand knowledge of the Wash, perhaps instead being based upon hearsay given to Adam of Croxton at Newark.

Ralph of Coggeshall's account is clearly the most logical, and therefore apparently the most reliable of the two. When viewed in the context that it was laid down around four years after the event, by a senior cleric from an order who had reason to dislike King John, a monarch who if anything, became less popular after death, there is certainly scope for the inclusion of bias against the King. Is it possible that the account also hides the King's assassination and theft of the crown jewels, by a joint Templar/Cistercian conspiracy?

The records of the chroniclers are the greatest sources of information available to us today to determine what happened in the past, they are in effect our history. The fact that they were laid down by holy men tends to put them above suspicion, but given the historical context, I do not think that their content should automatically be accepted as the unquestioned truth.

– 8 –
THE WEALTH
OF TEMPLE BRUER

———— • ————

If the Cistercian/Templar conspiracy theory were true, the question arises as to the fate of the misappropriated treasure.

There were four main Templar preceptories in Lincolnshire; Aslackby, Temple Bruer, Willoughton[63], and South Witham[64]. All were sited close to Roman roads, which would still have provided a strategic network in mediaeval times. Additionally the Templars had a smaller and less important preceptory at Mere, and an establishment at Eagle, which was effectively a hospital for old and infirm brethren[63]. There were also many other holdings, such as farms worked by lay brethren in the villages surrounding the preceptories.

English Templar preceptories were generally unfortified working farms, in many cases with a circular chapel based upon the proportions of the Temple of the Holy Sepulchre, in Jerusalem. Some were fortified to offer protection to people from baronial aggression; others had fortifications added later as the order grew in wealth for no practical reasons.

Preceptories were largely manned by only one or two actual knights, their sergeants (or esquires), and one or more chaplains. The rest of the occupants were lay brethren for menial work, and assorted craftsmen. Of these only the knights and some chaplains wore the white mantle and red cross, with which the order is associated; the remainder wore brown or black mantles with the red cross[61].

Willoughton is some 15 miles north of Lincoln and therefore a considerable distance from Swineshead. South Witham lies on the Great North Road between Stamford and Grantham, also a considerable distance from Swineshead. Aslackby and Temple Bruer are both 19 miles by road from Swineshead, assuming that the journey to each would be via Sleaford.

Having reached Sleaford one would turn south down Mareham Lane (Roman road) to get to Aslackby, or north across the heath land towards Lincoln, to get to Temple Bruer.

As the crow flies, Aslackby is slightly nearer to Swineshead, but the direct route in medieaval times would have crossed undrained inland fens, and as such would probably have been impassable.

It is a most curious fact that the small and isolated preceptory of Temple Bruer (Temple on the heath) was, at the time of the arrest of the Knights Templar in England, and subsequent seizure of their property by the crown, on 9th January 1308, the second wealthiest Templar establishment in England. At the time of the sequestration, Temple Bruer's income is recorded as £177, compared with £50 for the London Temple and £40 for Aslackby[63]. This wealth is generally attributed to wool production, but the Witham valley between Lincoln and Boston provided better grazing, as is evidenced by the number of sheep farming monastic settlements that existed there.

Furthermore, at the suppression of the Order, Temple Bruer was also the preceptory of the Grand Prior of all England, William de la More[64].

The suppression was carried out at the order of pope Clement V, but was first instigated by King Philip IV of France, who had alleged that various crimes of heresy, indecency and misconduct were institutionalised within the Order. It is generally thought that Philip's motive for making the allegations was really his jealousy of the Templars' tremendous wealth within France. Following the French arrests, the Pope, who was something of a puppet to the French Crown, was obliged to instruct the other European monarchs to follow suit, which some were reluctant to do, including King Edward II of England.

On 10th January 1308, the Sheriff of Lincolnshire, John de Cormel with twelve knights, arrested the Knights Templar of the Lincolnshire preceptories, including William de la More. They were imprisoned at *"Claxede"* (Clasketgate) in Lincoln[65].

William de la More was tried in Lincoln on 25th November 1309[66] in the Chapter House of the Cathedral[65] (the Chapter House being a ten

Figure 16: The Tower at Temple Bruer

sided meeting chamber similar in design to the Templars' own circular chapels). He refused to confess to any heresy or wrong doing within the order and was kept in open prison conditions until the arrival of two French Inquisitors (Dominican monks). He was then taken to the Tower of London where he was imprisoned and presumably tortured by the Inquisitors until his death in 1313[60].

The Inquisition was dispatched to England by Clement V, who disapproved of King Edward II's lenient treatment of the English Templars, who had fared a lot better than their French brethren, most of whom were tortured and some, including the order's Grand Master, Jacques de Molay, eventually burnt at the stake.

During his trial at Lincoln, William stated that he had been admitted to the preceptorship of Temple Bruer in 1300[66]. His very name, de la More, seems to have been taken from Temple Bruer (Bruer being derived from the French for Heath), which implies that it had always been his base, and for him to have reached the station of Grand Prior, it must have held some significance.

Temple Bruer is believed to have been founded around 1140, funded by a local landowner, William of Ashby[67] who became a Templar knight and bequeathed his estate to the order. The Bruer preceptory had manors in the local villages of Rowston, Kirkby, Brauncewell and Carlton, together with farmland in many of the other nearby villages[61].

Geographically there is no obvious reason why Temple Bruer should have held great importance. The main temple of the order in England was in London, and the main western powerbase of the organisation was in Paris. Someone as influential as the Grand Prior of all England would undoubtedly have spent a great deal of time in London, and would probably have travelled to the continent also. He is known to have been a trusted advisor to King Edward I, which suggests he spent time at court. Whilst Temple Bruer is sited on the Ermine Street, a Roman Road connecting Lincoln to London, it is still a fairly remote and distant location, and there were many preceptories much closer to the capital.

A further pointer to the status of Temple Bruer is the granting of royal consent in 1306 to the *"Militia of the Temple of England"* to *"make and crenellate a certain great and strong gate at their mansion of the Heath (de la Bruere) in Lincolnshire "[67]*, adding fortifications to what was essentially a farm and chapel.

The following is pure speculation, but it might be possible that Temple Bruer, amongst all the preceptories in England, was so wealthy and influential in 1308, because it housed, or had held, a secret wealth; the lost treasure of King John, acquired by the Templars some 90 years earlier.

In 1312, Temple Bruer, along with many other former Templar holdings (including Eagle and Willoughton in Lincolnshire), was officially handed to the Knights Hospitaller, for whom it was also important, as they designated it a commandery, a higher status than most of the houses and farms they held[63].

It would be ironic, should the Templar/Cistercian theory be true, that King Edward II may, in handing over Temple Bruer to the Hospitallers, have given them back the treasures they had passed to King John in 1216.

If any treasure was housed at Temple Bruer at the time of its seizure, it is most likely that it would have been confiscated by the crown. It is more likely however, that the Templars would already have moved it on, either at an earlier time to France, or once the Pope had ordered the arrest of the Templars, to Scotland.

The Knights Templar did not face arrest in Scotland in 1308, as the Scots King, Robert the Bruce, had been excommunicated by the Pope and therefore ignored the papal writ to seize the brethren and their assets. It is known that a number of the French Templars escaped the planned secret simultaneous dawn raids on Friday 13th October 1307, supposedly taking with them much of their wealth to Scotland and Portugal. Whilst the English order received more lenient treatment, it is possible that they also sought to preserve their most holy relics and valuable artefacts by moving them to safety, before they were confiscated.

Nothing of the fortified gate or the circular Templar chapel survives today, but a tower dating from around 1180[68], which was part of the complex of the chapel, still stands at Temple Bruer and is shown in Figure 15. There also remains a refectory hall built by the Hospitallers, which has been incorporated into a later farmhouse. The circular chapel would also have been used by the Hospitallers, who as a crusading order also constructed their chapels based upon the proportions of the Church of the Holy Sepulchre in Jerusalem.

There have been excavations at Temple Bruer by antiquarians, including the Rev. G. Oliver in 1837[69], and W. St. John Hope in 1907[67]. The former claimed to have found various macabre human remains in *"a perfect labyrinth of vaults, dungeons and intricate passages"*[69], attributed to brutal acts by the Knights Templar. The latter encountered undisturbed bedrock (except for steps leading to a crypt below the site of the circular chapel) in the locations of the previous supposed excavations, proving Oliver's claims to be fabrications.

W. St. John Hope's accounts always show a great deal of research into his subject matter, and his records of his own excavations are very well documented, but he makes no mention of the recovery of any valuable artefacts at Temple Bruer. The Rev. Oliver may have had a fanciful imagination with regard to recording things he did not really find, so I feel certain that had he found anything of value, he would not have resisted including mention of this, in his account of his excavation. It is therefore probably safe to say that if any treasure had once been stored at Temple Bruer, nothing of this remains today.

– **9** –

THE SWORD OF TRISTRAM

———— • ————

Whether or not my theory of Templar involvement in the death of King John and the loss of his treasure has any basis in fact, there is a further intriguing facet of the story that is worthy of mention. As previously noted, in the writings of A.V. Jenkinson[18], Empress Matilda's regalia included a sword known as the Sword of Tristram.

This is a fascinating inclusion, because Tristram, or Tristan, was a figure from Arthurian romance, not a mediaeval knight. It is also unusual in that it is a specifically named item, as compared with *"another sword"*, for instance. For these reasons I considered that if anything had survived the incident in the Wash, this sword would probably be the most traceable item.

The romance of Tristan and Isolde was written down in France around 1190, and may have been based on an earlier tale with a common ancestry to the similar tale of Lancelot and Guinevere. As with Lancelot, Tristan was appended to the Arthurian stories and appears as one of the named Knights of the Round Table in later Arthurian literature.

In the romance[70], Tristram's sword is central to the story, as it is damaged in a battle in which the King of Ireland is killed. The end of the sword is broken off, and this damage later betrays the identity of Tristram when he is sent to Ireland to collect the dead king's daughter, Isolde, for an arranged marriage with his uncle, King Mark of Devon.

Tristram falls in love with Isolde, they escape from Ireland and various complications follow, ending with the fleeing of Tristram to Brittany after Mark finds the lovers sleeping together and takes the sword, as a sign to Tristram that he knows of their treachery. The story of Tristram continues but the sword plays no further important part.

Further consideration is given to the origins of Tristram within this chapter, but first, an explanation of what importance the sword itself had in the time of King John is more relevant to this study.

Five swords were frequently included within mediaeval coronation ceremonies, and although these changed from time to time, they typically included the following; the King's Sword (his personal weapon), the Second Sword (also known as the Sword of Spiritual Justice), the Third Sword (also known as the Sword of Temporal Justice), the Sword of Mercy (also known as Curtana, the Sword of Ogier the Dane), and the Sword of State (a two handed sword exchanged with the King's own sword during the ceremony)[23].

From the descriptions of the mediaeval Sword of Mercy, and from the much later ornate ceremonial item given the same name (manufactured at some time in the eighteenth century along with ceremonial replacements for the Second and Third Swords, all three of which still exist), it is clear that this sword had a broken tip.

The damaged blade gives a logical reason why it must have been this sword that was associated with the heroic figure of Tristram. This association would in turn explain the alternate title of the Sword of Mercy, as Mark showed mercy to his nephew and his wife when he discovered their adultery, by taking the sword but not using it on the sleeping lovers.

It is likely that it was a mediaeval practice to associate ceremonial or ancient artefacts with heroic figures, to add to the perceived importance of the item, or to give it some symbolic value. This was after all common practice with bones and bits of wood of dubious origin, associated with remnants of saints and the true cross.

The withdrawal from Corfe Castle by King John is the last occasion (in mediaeval times) that I can find that the Sword of Mercy is referred to as the Sword of Tristram. The subsequently used name for the Sword of Mercy was Curtana, the Sword of Ogier the Dane.

Ogier also features in French romance; he was the son of the king of Denmark[71], and a military leader for Charlemagne. Ogier was about to take revenge on Charlemagne's son for the death of his own son (following an argument over a game of chess), when an angel appeared and struck his sword aside, breaking the tip and telling Ogier *"Mercy is better than revenge"*[72].

The title Curtana was used to describe a sword present when Henry III held a coronation ceremony for his Queen, Eleanor of Provence. The name Curtana is derived from the Latin word curtus, meaning short. Whether this was the same actual weapon as the Sword of Tristram, or whether different swords could be used almost as actors, to play ceremonial parts in the coronation proceedings, I am unable to determine.

Thus it can not be proven that the Sword of Tristram was lost in the Wash, and substituted by the Sword of Ogier the Dane, or that the sword survived the incident and was simply renamed in the course of time.

It is worth considering whether the Sword of Tristram belonged to an actual historical figure or was simply attributed to the figure of romance owing to the similarities of the blade. The themes in the romance date back to earlier legends of the Britons and Bretons, possibly as far back as the sixth century, along with many other stories upon which Arthurian lore is founded. The Welsh triad "Three Powerful Swineherds" has within it the characters Trystan, March, and Essyllt[73].

Arthurian scholars have associated Tristram/Tristan with Drystan of Cornwall, to whom a memorial stone still stands, two miles south of Castle Dore, which has long been linked in folklore with King Arthur. The (Latin) inscription on the stone reads, "*Drystan (Drustanus) lies here, son of Cunvawr*"[73]. "*Cynvawr*" is recorded as being the King of Dumnonia (Devon and Cornwall) by Gildas, a monk writing in 545[73].

It appears then that Tristram/Tristan may have been an actual historical character in addition to a figure of mediaeval romance, although it would seem unlikely that his sword would survive the intervening 650 years or so.

In twelfth century Europe, and France in particular, romancers told tales of chivalry and courtly love, which the old folk tales were easily adapted into. The widely known Arthur and his knights became an ideal vehicle for grouping old tales and new romances together in a popular contemporary format. However, many of the tales had pagan undertones, involving green men, magical cauldrons, severed heads, and sexuality, which didn't fit in too well with the ever-increasing power of the church. It is probably for this reason that the Vulgate Cycle of Arthurian tales was set down in around 1220 by the Cistercian monks[74].

The Vulgate Cycle repolarised Arthur and his knights towards Christian ideals, and in particular, the quest for the Holy Grail. The quest had featured previously in various versions of the tale of Percival, and the guardians of the grail were often described in mantles similar to those of the Templars, but in the Vulgate Cycle, they are explicitly named as the Knights Templar.

The Vulgate Cycle also names the castle in which the Grail is kept as the *"White Castle"*[74], which is of some interest as one of the Templars' strongholds in the Holy Lands was called Castel Blanc. The main tower and chapel of Castel Blanc are still largely intact. The castle was one of the strongest defensive positions in a chain of Templar castles along the Mediterranean cost, it is known in Arabic as Burj Safita, which means clear tower.

Whether or not this is an indication that their Cistercian brethren new the Templars to be in possession of legendary holy relics, such as the Grail and the bleeding lance, or to be the custodians of some sacred knowledge, as has been suggested by various authors over the years, is unknown, and is not the subject of this research. That the Templars carried out archaeological excavations beneath the Temple of Solomon in Jerusalem is widely accepted, and that they had a significant collection of holy relics and treasures is undoubted, as such objects were collected by all pious religious orders.

A sword, itself a symbol of the Templars, named after one of Arthur's now holy knights, would I suspect, have been something that the Templars could have accommodated in their treasury or reliquary with enthusiasm, whether originally belonging to the Tristram of old, or Ogier the Dane, or a contemporary weapon which had become associated with Tristram owing to its missing tip.

This of course is pure speculation, but may offer a further pointer towards Templar involvement in the disappearance of King John's treasure, and provide a reason as to why the name of the sword used as the Sword of Mercy in state ceremonies changed following John's collection of the weapon as part of Empress Matilda's Regalia, from Corfe Castle in the summer of 1216.

–10–
TREASURE HUNTERS
———•———

Full research of the subject of King John's lost treasure would not be complete without a review of those earlier researchers and adventurers who, having considered possible locations for the loss of the treasure, have gone on to try and physically locate and retrieve it.

I have no doubt there have been many individual unrecorded efforts by field walkers and metal detectorists, and I know of one site where organised metal detecting events have taken place, but there have also been some highly organised attempts, records of which are covered in this final chapter, bringing this 800 year old story right up to date.

The beauty of searching for items in an area which was, until near modern times, a tidal estuary, is that there should be no archaeological 'clutter' to confuse the searcher. There are not likely to be any bronze or iron age finds (although offerings such as swords and axes are known to have been placed ceremonially in water by our forebears). There should be no Roman, Saxon, Viking or Mediaeval age finds unless from a boat which failed to navigate the estuary.

Logically, apart from the possibility of King John's baggage train, there should be no finds predating the reclamation of the various portions of land, and in the central part of the delta until the creation of Wingland in the 1820s.

An additional benefit when searching with equipment such as resistivity meters or ground penetrating radar is that geologically, the soils within the estuary are fairly uniform. Centuries of fine sediments of silts and sand have been laid down without any major anomalies, except perhaps occasional trees washed down by the river following times of upland flooding.

Whilst on the subject of geology, it is worth mentioning the site investigation boreholes for the railway line and Cross Keys bridge, carried out in 1887, by the Great Northern Railway[75]. These show silt to a depth of 23 feet (7m), below which lies a band of sand and shells. There are various other strata below this with the bores terminating at 64 feet (19.5m). It is likely that any treasure or goods, would lay in the top 23 feet, which was built up by the annual accretion of silts within the estuary, washed down from the fens inland at times of flood. It is not thought likely that any objects settling through self-weight would be able to sink into the strata beneath the silt.

Perhaps the earliest treasure hunter story relates to Robert, 3rd Lord Tiptoft (or Baron Tybetot) of Suffolk (1341 to 1372). It is rumoured that Robert suddenly rose to the status of a wealthy man having recovered the lost treasure from the Wash. However, Robert's father, John, 2nd Lord Tybetot was heir to a large number of estates throughout the midlands and in the south of England, acquired by his family during the 1260s. His mother was the daughter of Baron Badlesmere and the Norman-Irish Countess Margaret de Clare[76], who apart from being an influential woman and wealthy heiress in her own right had married two wealthy husbands. Robert himself married into the influential Deincourt family, so, all things considered he was likely to have been a very rich individual. I am unsure of the root of the rumours regarding his sudden financial gains and can find no reference material to substantiate the idea.

Evidently the rumours around Robert Tiptoft did not become too well known, as the belief that the treasure is there to be found has endured to modern times. In the early twentieth century it was said by some to lie hidden in "King John's Hole", a dank pool somewhere just south of the road between Lynn and Long Sutton[77].

An organised attempt to locate and recover the treasure commenced in 1929, when the Crown granted a licence permitting 420 acres (170ha) of the Wingland Estate to be researched by a group known as the Wash Committee[78]. This group consisted of Sir William Muirhead (an engineer), Mr Curnock (a journalist) and a Mr d'Avigdor. In 1930 they also gained a licence from the Ministry of Fisheries to search a further 1,100 acres (445ha) on the Sutton Bridge Estate[79].

In 1932 an American professor, James R. Herbert Boone, gave up his post in humanities at the John Hopkins University in Baltimore, to come to England and join in the search. Prof Boone offered to back the Wash

Committee with £40,000, and the Fen Research Limited Company was established.

In the same year, a licence was secured to search a further 5,470 acres (2,214ha) in the Sutton Grange Area[11]. The Company was able to offer farmers and land lords 10 shillings per acre of land surveyed and £10 per acre for any land on which excavations were carried out.

The Company employed a gentleman called E. Gaspard Ponsonby on a well-paid three year contract, to act as their agent, but in Sept 1933, after his first year, Ponsonby was dismissed having followed Boone to Rome to request a further £30,000 funding. A court case for wrongful dismissal ensued and the company became known nationally as a result of the publicity of that case[79].

It is interesting that one of the surveying techniques adopted by the Company in their search, was divining. In June 1933 Boone met with a Charles Gladitz who claimed to have located the baggage train using a needle through a cork. Gladitz claimed to have identified the exact location of a ten mile long column of dead men, horses and carts. Specifically, he claimed to have located 24 carts, one of which he asserted was heavier than the others and was therefore likely to have been carrying the king's treasury[79].

It would seem that the claims of Mr Gladitz proved to be false and the dreams of Mr Boone remained unrealised, because in 1936, the Company went into liquidation with little, if any, excavation having actually been carried out since its establishment in 1932 (no £10 payments to farmers having ever been made).

In 1935, a Tom Crowder of Bardney contacted Fen Research Limited to inform them that they were searching in the wrong area[80]. He claimed that a friend had a spoon bearing the monogram of King John, found in Boston some 50 years earlier. Unfortunately the spoon could not be produced as it had been left in the drawer of a table which had been sold. The fact that the existence of the spoon cannot be verified at all, let alone the authenticity of the monogram it is said to have carried, means that this tale does not offer any credible contribution to the story.

Professors James Holt (mediaeval history) and David Evans (geology) of the University of Nottingham's Wash Research Committee, attempted to prove the existence of a causeway, at a theoretical high tide line, by means of site investigation bores, somewhere between Sutton Bridge and Wisbech in 1956[81].

In the transcript of a 1963 BBC broadcast[82], the professors claim to have sunk four bores, the fourth of which struck an impenetrable object or stratum at a depth of fifteen feet (4.57m), which was not encountered in the other holes. Spoil from the cutter was taken back to Nottingham for analysis, and according to the professors, was found to contain fragments of copper and silver, and a fragment of gold, together with ferrous objects, suspected to be nails. They concluded that evidence of the treasure had been found.

A former student of archaeology contacted me in 2004[83] having read the first edition of this book, to inform me that during his time at the University of Nottingham in the 1970s, he had spoken to a laboratory technician who recalled that traces of metals had been found in one of the bore hole samples. Attempts to trace any former members of staff who might be able to verify the story have, so far, proved unsuccessful; certainly the technician named by my correspondent retired some 30 years ago.

The odds of striking the treasure in such a large area with one of four trial bores are literally incredible, and attempts by the author to get the University of Nottingham to verify the findings, or to prove the existence of the metal fragments, have proved fruitless; they can find no reference to the claims whatsoever. The discovery of fragments of gold would surely have been followed up by a thorough archaeological excavation. The value of recovered finds would have been inestimable, in academic, heritage and financial terms.

The site of the Holt/Evans ground investigation is understandably not disclosed, except for mention of an orchard. A gentleman I spoke to in March 2004 remembers seeing the investigation take place, and described the location to me, as it took place within half a mile of the farm on which he grew up, on the Norfolk side of the River Nene on a line between Walpole and Tydd Gote. I estimate the site was just south of Marsh Road at Walpole Marsh (Ordnance Survey Grid Reference TF 487 174), where older Ordnance Survey maps indicate an orchard.

This location is just 500yards to the west of what would have been a small promontory in the line of Roman Bank, and it corresponds with Holt's proposal that the crossing point was on a line between Walpole and Tydd Gote (as mentioned previously in Chapter 2)

In prof. Holt's own paper on the subject of King John's treasure[13], written in 1961 (after the site investigation but before the BBC broadcast), he very briefly mentions carrying out the bore holes with prof. Evans, but makes no mention of any metal fragments, or anything else, being recovered, and states that the site investigation was not related to a search for the treasure.

Clearly there is some discrepancy surrounding the issue of the recovered metal fragments, and on balance of the evidence available, I have to suggest that the claims made by the professors in the radio broadcast were, for whatever reason, grossly exaggerated or entirely false.

The development of a more recent rumour surrounding the treasure was perhaps inevitable. The construction of Sutton Bridge gas fired power station in 1999, by American company Enron at a cost of £337m, has led to speculation that the site of the power station was chosen to allow recovery of the treasure during construction, and its subsequent smuggling to America. A conspiracy theory further fuelled by the fact that Enron sold the structure to English company EDF Energy, as soon as it had been commissioned.

According to a radio broadcast (Dec. 2001) William Smethurst and Jacqueline McGlade attempted to locate the baggage train using low level aircraft flights with ground penetrating radar techniques. Their attempt was not successful, but as discussed in Chapter 2 they were searching over the Welland rather than the Wellstream.

At the time I started marketing the first edition of this book (July 2003), I was told that the granddaughter of Mr Boone, the American financier of Fen Research Limited, had spoken to people in the Swineshead area[84] claiming that she still retained the rights to excavate under the original licences granted in the 1930s. I heard a further rumour that she planned to excavate in the Sutton Bridge area that summer.

My attempts to trace Mr Boone's granddaughter at that time and subsequently have failed. I did however discover that some exploratory bores were carried out, in both 2003 and 2004, but these appear not be associated with her.

In 2003 Walton Hornsby and Philip Haydn-Slater set out to find the treasure. Their exploits are recorded in a documentary which can be viewed on the internet[85]. Hornsby and Haydn-Slater recruited dowsing expert Jim Longton to identify the location of the baggage train, and the exact location of individual carts and specific items of regalia, using a divining rod.

It is fascinating that this is the second recorded serious attempt to find the treasure which has utilised divining as a search technique.

The location is (understandably, given the motives of the expedition) not openly disclosed in the documentary, although clues from the background of the film footage would indicate it took place in August or September, between the old and new A17 routes in the parish of Sutton Bridge (Lincolnshire) at Ordnance Survey Grid Reference TF 464 321.

Two 100mm diameter percussive bore holes were sunk to a depth of seven metres but, other than a few fragments of wooden material which one might expect within river sediment, nothing was recovered.

Norfolk County Council hold a record of a more extensive bore hole survey carried out in the Norfolk parish of Walpole in 2004[86]. This is recorded as being within Ordnance Survey Grid square TF 47 16, although text of the report itself implies that it may have taken place in Lincolnshire.

The report states that Ian Wallace conducted a metal detector survey in the Tydd Gote area, Tydd Gote being within Lincolnshire just to the north of the location where Cambridgeshire, Norfolk and Lincolnshire adjoin each other.

Wallace identified an area with a high metallic concentration at some depth, and commissioned in excess of 30 bore holes to a depth of six metres.

No finds were made, but some samples of the sediments included deposits from iron rich soils, and also small (20mm long) fragments, thought at first to be wood, but on analysis found to be iron mineral concretions, which can develop naturally around wooden fragments or other organic matter during the process of decomposition[86].

When one considers the sources of the rivers Nene and Great Ouse in Northamptonshire, and the iron rich geology through which they pass on their course to the Wash, it is not surprising that the deposits in the former Wellstream estuary are fairly rich in iron content. Surprising perhaps, that these are significant enough to trigger detection with a metal detector though, and one has to question if similar fragments to these are the real explanation for the earlier claims of Professors Holt and Evans to have recovered metallic fragments, although it would account for ferrous content only, not for copper, silver or gold.

After publishing the first edition, I was contacted by a farmer, who is also a marine salvage contractor, who claims to know exactly where the treasure is located, and to have documentary proof of this location. However, with his salvage expertise and contacts in the farming community, which ought to make excavation easier for him than most, he has not yet substantiated his claims with evidence[87].

Having looked into the organised searches and logs of all archaeological finds in the vicinity, it is evident that no verifiable find which can be linked to the lost treasure is known to have been made. However, there are a few artefacts connected with the story, which are worthy of mention.

The most significant artefact is the stunning King John Cup, housed in the Regalia Room at the Old Gaol House in King's Lynn. Pictured in Figure 18, the cup is a magnificent piece with enamelled friezes, and is without doubt a national treasure.

The cup is reputed to have been given to Lynn by King John together with a crusader sword in 1204 when he granted the town its charter and status of free burgh[88]. It is the earliest known surviving piece of secular plate[89]. As might be expected in the circumstances, folklore has given the cup an alternative history; that it is an item recovered from the lost treasure.

However, some experts now believe that neither of these pedigrees is correct, as the style and workmanship have been suggested as being fourteenth century. Quite rightly, in my view, the people of King's Lynn dispute this questioning of part of their heritage, and it will always remain the King John Cup.

Whatever the true origin of the King John Cup, it does give some insight into the possible quality and magnificence of the items lost. The use of the word "treasure" is clearly not an exaggeration.

In 1882, a hoard of 60 to 70 coins was found in a Mr Naylor's field at Sutton Crosses[90] and although the coins turned out to be from the reigns of Edward IV and Richard III in the fifteenth century, this find must have aroused a great deal of interest in the lost treasure story at the time. I would expect that My Naylor's field was on the landward side of Roman Bank, as the bank was still the tidal defence at Sutton Crosses in the fifteenth century.

An interesting story of another artefact associated with the treasure was reported in the Daily Express in 1906, after the discovery of what was called an *"ancient loving cup"*[19]. Approximately 200mm tall, it was said to bear the date 1162 and was supposedly made of silver. It was sold by the finder to a jeweller who later identified it as the pewter bottom to a ship's moderator lamp, the date being in fact the design registration number. I do not know of the whereabouts of this item today, or if it was kept at all.

During my research, I was also told a story of a chalice reputedly found in the Gedney Drove End area in about 1990. The artefact was said to have been found and reported by a farmer, and was then taken away to the British Museum. However Lincolnshire County Council's Sites and Monuments Record[4] have no record of such an item being reported, and a search of the British Museum's inventory of finds from Lincolnshire[91] produced nothing resembling a mediaeval goblet or chalice. It is likely that this find is fictitious, or it may be a modern re-telling of the *"ancient loving cup"* story above.

In 2007 I was contacted by an American called Dean Smith. Dean had read my book and sent me an old family account of the discovery of a religious cross known as the Priestly Cross (pictured in Figure 17), as he wondered if the cross could be connected to the lost treasure.

The cross was found by Dean's ancestor, John Priestley, who worked as a shepherd and lived in a hamlet near Boston in around 1820. *"When walking home from work one evening, John went through a portion of the Abbey that was in ruins; it had been destroyed by Cromwell. He spied a glint of gold under the edge of a stone which he lifted and found that it was a beautiful gold cross. He gave it to his girlfriend, Ann Benn, who later became his wife. "*[92]. Ann was Dean's great, great grandmother. Unfortunately, neither the hamlet nor the abbey are named.

Following the dissolution of the monasteries after 1536, many abbeys fell into disrepair, and it is known that the masonry from the ruins of Swineshead Abbey was taken and re-used as early as 1607 by Sir John Lockton for building his own manor house, so it is unlikely that the Priestley Cross was found there, but not impossible as there are still undulations in the ground which might have had masonry visible in 1820.

Dean's family have had the cross examined by a jeweller who has determined it is made from a gold alloy rather than pure gold. My first thought was that as it does not depict Christ on the cross, it is more likely to be Protestant than Catholic, which would place it well beyond the life and times of King John. On closer inspection, it appears to be a casting rather than a hand crafted object, as there are lesser quality finished edges around the eyelet for the chain link and one or two other edges.

Advice from Westminster Abbey and from Lincoln's museum, The Collection[93], indicate that the style of the cross is likely to be of the Georgian or even the Victorian period, although the latter would not tally with the date it is said to have been found. Perhaps John Priestley found something which had only just been lost. In any instance, there is no connection with King John's treasure.

To sum up this chapter, despite the best efforts of researchers and treasure hunters, both amateur and organised (the unlikely rumours surrounding Robert Tiptoft, and claims of professors Holt and Evans notwithstanding), and regardless of the interesting stories surrounding the various objects described above, no single artefact has ever been known to have been found which can be associated with the loss of the treasure in the Wellstream estuary[94].

When all the intrusive activities surrounding the cutting of the new River Nene outfall, intensive agriculture, the cutting of drains and building of dykes, the construction of roads, banks, farms, and the village of Sutton Bridge are considered along with the activities of the treasure hunters, all without yielding a find, one has to question if the treasure is there to be found at all.

Figure 17: Priestley Cross

Figure 18: The King John Cup

– **11** –
HISTORY OR MYSTERY?

———— • ————

If one accepts the chronicler's accounts, King John's treasure was lost in a poorly executed crossing of the Wellstream estuary on 12th October 1216, and the King was coincidentally taken ill with dysentery or food poisoning at Swineshead Abbey on the same or the following evening, subsequently dying at Newark in the early hours of 19th October 1216. This is history as it has been given to us by near contemporary monastic scribes.

This series of events, when viewed in context with King John's struggles for survival against a range of pressing enemies, his lack of popularity, his financial problems, and the biases and discrepancies exhibited by the chroniclers (who were not evidently present at the incident), must be viewed with some suspicion.

The question of why the King collected his treasury together so soon after Magna Carta, and then transported it around the countryside with him, must be asked. Presumably because he was afraid of it falling into the hands of his enemies, or perhaps it was because he planned to tax the custodian orders in the immediate future, and would then have to add them to the list of people he could not trust.

Certainly he needed capital to hand to pay for his spiralling defensive campaign against the Barons and the Dauphin of France, the accidental loss of the treasure being an excuse for its misappropriation (this you will recall formed my Conspiracy Theory No.1).

It can be concluded from the chroniclers and the Itinerary of the King[40] (subject to the King himself not being directly involved in disposing of the treasure) that the King was not present at the time of the supposed incident, having travelled round the estuary via Wisbech, instead of directly across it. It can be interpreted from the chronicles that no one survived the incident, and that the King was not informed of the loss until reaching Swineshead Abbey.

The baggage train may have been deliberately waylaid whilst separated from King John, or misguided on the crossing by local guides possibly under the instruction of one of the King's enemies such as the local dispossessed noble, Robert de Gresley. The motives of gaining military advantage, or simply of plunder, are clear and would explain the lack of survivors (Conspiracy Theory No.2).

Local folklore places the death of the King on the shoulders of Brother Simon, a Cistercian monk at Swineshead Abbey, who acted in the interest of the greater good. If this were true, the monks of Swineshead, possibly in collusion with others such as Robert de Gresley, may have appropriated treasure after the act, although this would seem unlikely (Conspiracy Theory No.3).

The accounts of King John's journey from Lynn to Newark, do not note the point at which King's retinue of mounted knights parted company from him. They do note that the King's corpse was virtually stripped of everything, and that travellers were seen leaving Newark with laden packhorses on the morning of his death.

This may be a hint that the treasure along with everything else was simply stolen from the King after his death, by his own household staff, bodyguard, or other paid forces. The Wellstream story may then have been devised to backdate the loss of the treasure, and explain away the low numbers of remaining personnel.

Alternatively, the mounted knights may have been responsible for the disappearance of the treasure somewhere on route, the remaining theft of personal effects at Newark being an unplanned act by members of his household staff (Conspiracy Theory No.4). This series of events would suggest a natural cause of death for King John was possible, but the scale of the theft could not have been kept secret, as the knights would have been drawn from all over the country, unless the robbery was orchestrated by a single powerful individual such as William the Marshall.

That William Shakespeare was aware of the poisoning legend in 1596, some 380 years after the event, is I think one of the most important and fascinating details in the story, as it implies that the local legends surrounding Brother Simon are of great age and significance, supported by earlier documented accounts, going back at least to William Caxton in 1480. The survival of the effigy purported to depict Brother Simon gives further credence to the tale.

Brother Simon, if it is he who is depicted in the effigy, was not a Cistercian monk, but a crusader knight. The discrepancy between his appearance and his monastic title cannot have gone un-noticed by those who have, over the centuries, retained the association with his name. If he were a Templar knight, a member of an order with close links to the Cistercian monks, he would have been addressed as Brother.

That the Templars were involved in an assassination plot would on the face of things seem unlikely, but cannot be dismissed as impossible. They were certainly collectors of wealth needed to support their ventures in the Holy Lands, and also pious collectors of religious artefacts. They had further motives associated with the preservation of their Cistercian brethren. It should also be remembered that the Templars were answerable directly to the Pope, who undoubtedly favoured the French Crown above the other European monarchs, thus the early removal of King John would have saved the French from having to continue a costly campaign in England (Conspiracy Theory No.5), although they in fact remained until routed in Lincoln in May 1217.

This Templar/Cistercian conspiracy theory, whilst circumstantial, ties up many loose ends. It provides a possible destination for the treasure as the disproportionate wealth and influence of the Knights Templar in the vicinity is evident and largely unexplained. It provides an explanation for the coincident death of the King and disappearance of his treasure. It provides an explanation of why Brother Simon's effigy is that of a crusader knight and not a monk. It offers a motive for Brother Simon's actions and explains how local legends surrounding the poisoning of the King have evolved, and hence where William Shakespeare and William Caxton's versions of the King's death originated (which would otherwise have been somewhat bizarre when compared to the events recorded by the chroniclers). The theory also offers an explanation of why the Cistercian Ralph of Coggeshall's chronicle differs so much from that of the Benedictine Roger of Wendover.

Ultimately the theory explains why, to date, no finds have ever been identified which offer any proof whatsoever that the story of King John's treasure being lost in the Wash is a historical fact.

That no proof exists of the survival to modern times of any of the artefacts supposedly lost in the Wash, does not categorically mean that they were lost in the Wash, only that no recognisable mention of them can be found.

The goods may have been traded at any subsequent time and fallen into the hands of people who were unaware of their pedigree, or were interested in their monetary value alone. It is likely that they would have eventually been shipped abroad or melted down. The Knights Templar had an established international banking system, and the movement of funds was commonplace, it is likely that particularly valuable items were exported to France.

Events such as the arrest of the Templars, the dissolution of the monasteries, and the English Civil War, all add to the likelihood that any treasure appropriated by the Templars in England is almost certain not to have survived.

The continued use of the Sword of Tristram in state ceremonies is an intriguing anomaly and implies either that the sword survived the incident or was not part of the treasury transported by the King, or more likely that it was superseded by another broken tipped sword which assumed the earlier sword's identity and symbolic purpose.

Whilst I cannot offer any irrefutable evidence to support my theory, I remain highly sceptical that the suspicious death of King John and the loss of his treasure were two separate events linked only by the fact that they occurred at an almost simultaneous point in time. It is my firm belief that these events were closely linked and indeed carefully orchestrated.

Furthermore, it has become my belief as this research has unfolded, that the Cistercian monks and their brethren the Knights Templar were

Figure 19: The Wash

involved in this series of events. Together they had the motives, means and backing to dispose of the King, and acquire his treasure into the bargain.

Unless the fields of Wingland, which now overlay the muddy Wellstream estuary, yield some find contemporary with the period, be it a magnificent treasure or simply a mundane horse fitting, I remain sceptical of the accounts of the chroniclers of 1220, and their tale that King John's treasure was lost in the Wash on the 12th of October 1216.

Figure 20: The Wash

BIBLIOGRAPHY AND REFERENCES

Ref:

1   Treasure Hunt: N. Warren, from Fortean Times FT128 (1999)
2   The Changing Fenland: H.C. Darby
3   British Geological Survey: Sheet 145 (1978)
4   Sites and Monuments Record: Lincolnshire County Council
5   The Mediaeval Fenland: H.C. Darby
6   The Concise Oxford Dictionary of Place Names
7   History of Long Sutton and District: E.W. and B.A. Robinson (1981)
8   The Vancouver Times (10 Oct 1864)
9   Pre-1830 maps of The Wash:
    i.   Camden's Britannia, Gough edition (1789)
    ii. Hayward (1604)
    iii. Speed (1611)
    iv. Vermuyden (1642)
    v.   Badeslade (1723)
    vi. Kinderley (1751)
    vii. Cory (1793)
    viii. Watson (1825)
    ix. Gough (c1360)
10 Lincolnshire: A. Mee (1949)
11 King John's Treasure: G. Fowler (1953)
12 Nineteenth Century Local Historians:
    i.   Walker and Craddock (1849)
    ii. Marshall (1859)
    iii. Gardiner (1859)
13 King John's Disaster in the Wash: J.C. Holt (1961)
14 King John's Treasure: BBC Radio 4 broadcast (11/18 Dec. 2001)
15 Woken's Eye: W. Smethurst (1999)
16 King John's Treasure: S.A. English (1954)
17 Church, Charter and Crown: Pre-Reformation 1199-1230: M. Bell (2004)

18   The Jewels Lost in The Wash: A.V. Jenkinson (1923)
19   The Fens: A. Bloom
20   The Itinerary of King John of England: T.D. Hardy (1827)
21   H.E.Hallam, quoted from a talk in 1954: The Lincolnshire Echo (30 Mar. 2004)
22   Matthew Paris, from Chronica Majora (circa 1259)
23   The Crown Jewels and Other Regalia in the Tower of London: Major-Gen. H.D.W. Sitwell (1953)
24   King John: The Stories of Lost Treasure and the Death of a King: W. McConnell (2004)
25   The Life and Times of King John: M. Ashley (1972)
26   The Minority Of Henry III: D. A. Carpenter (1990)
27   www.catherinehanley.co.uk/historical-background/nicola-de-la-haye
28   King John: W.L. Warren
29   The Quest for King John's Long-Lost Treasure – Sucked Down by the Whirlpool: J. Wright (2008)
30   Roger of Wendover, from Flores Historiarum (circa 1220)
31   Major W. Anstruther-Gray, quoted in The Loss of King John's Baggage Train in the Wellstream in October 1216: W.H. St. John-Hope (1906)
32   Ralph of Coggeshall, from Chronicon Anglicanum (circa1220)
33   i. C. Reid, quoted in The Loss of King John's Baggage Train in the Wellstream in October 1216: W.H. St. John-Hope (1906)
      ii. Proudman Oceanographic Laboratory, quoted in BBC Radio 4 broadcast, King John's Treasure (11/18 Dec. 2001)
34   King John's Lost Treasure and the Templars: S. Mortimer (2006)
35   Personal correspondence: N. Panting (June 2003)
36   Personal correspondence: M. Bell (Mar. 2004)
37   A History of Swineshead: P.A. Southworth (1996)
38   Swineshead: Rev. J.G.H. Cragg
39   The History of Crowland Abbey: R. Gough (1816)
40   King John: W. Shakespeare (circa 1596)
41   Holinshed's Chronicles as used in Shakespeare's Plays: Ed. Prof. A. and J. Nicoll (1927)
42   William Caxton, from Fructus Temporum (1480)
43   John Foxe's Book of Martyrs: J. Foxe (1583 edition)
44   Personal correspondence: B. Varlow (Oct 2005)
45   A History of the County of Lincoln (Vol 2): Dawson (1906)
46   www.tudorplace.com.ar/Talboys
47   i Highways and Byways in Lincolnshire: W.F. Rawnsley (1914)
      ii A Short History of Lincolnshire: I.C. Brears (1927)

48 Personal correspondence: R. Mouraille (Aug. 2005)
49 An Account of the Descovery of King John: V. Greene (1797)
50 Personal correspondence: D. Morrison (Sept 2005).
51 Poem: J. Bale (1529)
52 Personal correspondence: P. Stapleton (July 2003)
53 Legends of the Fenland People: C. Marlowe (1926)
54 Portrait of Lincolnshire: M. Lloyd (1983)
55 The owner of the property on which the effigy of Brother Simon now resides (who wishes to remain anonymous)
56 Early Secular Effigies in England (The Thirteenth Century): H.A. Tummers (1980)
57 Personal correspondence: Prof. M.C. Barber (2000)
58 The Buildings of England (Lincolnshire): N. Pevsner and J. Harris (1964)
59 www.web-site.co.uk/knights_templar: N.Worthington (2000)
60 The Templars: P.P. Reid (1999)
61 The Knights Templar: Major J.W. Collinson, from the Journal of the Royal Air Force College (1930)
62 Supremely Abominable Crimes (The trial of the Knights Templar): E. Burman (1994)
63 i.   Mediaeval Religious Houses: D.Knowles and R. Neville Hadcock
   ii. Records of the Templars in England in the Twelfth Century: B.A.Lees (1935)
64 The Knights of Temple Bruer and Aslackby: A. White (1981)
65 The Knights Templar in Kesteven: Dr.D. Mills
66 Temple Bruer: Prof. R.de la Bere, from the Lincolnshire Magazine (1936)
67 The Round Church of the Knights Templar at Temple Bruer, Lincolnshire: W.H. St. John-Hope (1908)
68 Temple Bruer and Lincoln Heath (Nr.Cranwell): Capt.W.A. Cragg, from the R.A.F. Cadet College Magazine (1927)
69 On Temple Bruer and its Knights: Rev. Dr. G. Oliver (1841)
70 The Illustrated Encyclopaedia of Arthurian Legends: R. Coghlan (1993)
71 Legends of Charlemagne: T. Bulfinch (quoted at www.bulfinch.org/legends)
72 Crown Jewels: A. Beutel and R. Jahner (quoted at www.rtb-nord.uni-hannover.de)
73 The Quest for Arthur's Britain: ed. G. Ashe (1968)
74 The Search for the Grail: G. Phillips (1995)
75 A. Ross, quoted in The Loss of King John's Baggage Train in the Wellstream in October 1216: W.H. St. John-Hope (1906)

76   www.thepeerage.com
77   The Norfolk and Suffolk Coast: W. A. Dutt (1909)
78   Boston Guardian (8 Feb. 1936), quoted in Swineshead Remembers:
      P.A. Southworth (1999)
79   The Sunday Times (5 Aug 1934)
80   The Lincolnshire Echo (3 Jan. 1933)
81   i.   The Great Treasure Hunts: Furneaux (1969)
      ii. The Daily Telegraph (8 Oct. 1956)
82   Shire Talk: Transcript of BBC Radio Programme (1963)
83   Personal correspondence: W. Radford (Mar.2004)
84   Personal correspondence: P.A. Southworth (June 2000)
85   The Search for the Treasure of King John: A. Humphreys (2003)
86   Norfolk County Council: Heritage Explorer Ref 40716
87   Personal correspondence: D. Tonge (July 2003)
88   Fenland Rivers: I. Wedgewood
89   Glittering Prospects: J. Allen (1975)
90   Lincolnshire County Council   www.lincstothepast.com Ref
      MLI22328
91   www.thebritishmuseum.ac.uk
92   Introduction to an Ancestor: A. Brothers (from personal
      correspondence D. Smith) (Dec 2007)
93   Personal correspondence: J. Rawlinson, Museum Supervisor at
      Westminster Abbey and A. Lee of The Collection (June 2014)
94   Sites and Monuments Records:
      i.   Lincolnshire County Council
      ii. Cambridgeshire County Council
      iii. Norfolk County Council

Other sources of reference:
John Lackland: K. Northgate (1902)
The Reign of King John: S. Painter (1949)
King John: J.C. Holt (1963)
An Historical Account of the Ancient Town of Wisbech: W. Watson
(1827)
The Book of the Magna Carta: G. Hindley (1990)
Camden's Britannia: (translation 1805)
E. Hall: Local Tour Guide (1996)
Worcester Cathedral Guide Booklet (1999)
A History of England: K. Feiling (1950)

INDEX